Changing Career to Change Your Life

Kathleen Houston

TROTMAN

About the author

Kathleen Houston is an experienced Careers Adviser working both with young people in schools and colleges and with adult jobseekers. Having experienced the common problems of many career returners after her own rather long career break, she researched effective jobseeking strategies with employers nationally and regionally. Her research worked in a personal way as she gained employment herself, winning not one, but two part-time contracts to suit her personal and family circumstances.

She is committed to helping people improve their chances of success and finds her work fascinating and rewarding. Kathleen has also been involved in CV and jobsearch workshops in her role as an adult guidance worker with a Lancashire college and she writes regularly on jobseeking issues. Most recently she has been an expert on national radio helping the long-term unemployed with advice and support. She is also the author of *Getting into Job Opportunities* and *Creating Winning CVs & Applications*, both published by Trotman.

This first edition published in 2000 by Trotman and Company Ltd
2 The Green, Richmond, Surrey TW9 1PL

© *Trotman and Company Limited 2000*

British Library Cataloguing in Publication Data
A catalogue record for this book is available from the British Library

ISBN 0 85660 532 8

All rights reserved. No part of this publication may be reproduced, stored in
a retrieval system or transmitted in any form or by any means, electronic and mechanical,
photocopying, recording or otherwise without prior permission
of Trotman and Company Ltd.

Typeset by Midlands Book Typesetting Company, Loughborough
Printed and bound in Great Britain by
Creative Print and Design (Wales), Ebbw Vale.

Contents

An important dedication
This book is dedicated to the ones I love, who will all know who they are.
I would not be what I am today but for my Mum and Dad,
so they deserve a special mention.
I would not be able to do what I do today without the person that I offload
everything on to, my darling husband John, who also drives me crazy!

Introduction

A philosophical discourse, the meaning of life and what is really out there

There's a Zen-style story about an old lady on a bus journey: every five minutes she asks the driver to tell her when she will reach the bus terminus. She begins to irritate the driver with her persistency. She spends the whole journey in anxious expectation and drives everyone around her crazy. She arrives in the end, frazzled and weary. The philosophical point to the story is the old chestnut: 'she missed the fun of the journey in the stress of wondering when she would arrive.'

Two-thirds of our lives are taken up by the job we do and, somewhat surprisingly, many of us spend the whole life journey stuck on the same bus wondering when it will all be over, when we could simply have enjoyed the passing of time, changed buses, taken the train, walked for a bit, or simply got off the bus! It ought to be that simple, but a thousand different chains hold us back and we fight to stay in the same place, 'stuck on the bus whimpering, staring at the blurry scenery' rather than stepping into the unknown.

But life these days is about change, whether it is surviving, accepting or embracing change. The idea of change can be exciting and stimulating but as a general rule we resist the challenge. We rarely seek change in our lives. While our present situation is comfortable, or simply bearable, we trudge along, but for many their situation can become so intolerable or impossible that change is forced upon them. At that point we accelerate into super-panic mode and have to deal with the double stress of having to make possibly painful change without really understanding all our options.

Some kind of career change at some point in life is almost inevitable these days, and many people realise now that second, third or even fourth chances are available. Reading this book will help you see and fully understand what is out there for you and how you can make the career change you choose – the perfect answer to your situation. This book will show you how to look positively on voluntary or forced career change and make it work for you.

The book is a mixture of easy, practical advice and personal career management philosophy; it can be dipped into or read as a whole, so feel free to turn to the most relevant section for you. However, you may find that the book has more to offer you as a whole and that, read as a whole, it has a more galvanising effect on you by changing the way you think about yourself and the belief systems you have about what is really out there for you. A good starting point is the Career Change Menu in Chapter 1, so begin by finding yourself in this list and then work through the Quick Answers to focus on the misguided thinking and 'mental bruises' that are holding you back from the mega-fulfilling career of your dreams. Be warned, though, that once you realise how illusory the chains are that bind you to your present situation, you will have no excuses for not taking the first steps to making dreams a reality.

CHAPTER 1

You really can change your life

One of the best reasons for taking the time to contemplate a restaurant menu is the anticipation that comes with visualising or mentally tasting the menu items. For some people the nutritional value of the different menu combinations or the cost of different meals might also come into it, but for the most part it is probably an instinctive choice with a little bit of reasoning thrown in. With this Career Change Menu, it is infinitely preferable for you to go with an instinctive choice, because it is more than likely the truest response. However dreary the picture it creates, it will confirm our starting point and, in the process, clarify for you the need or urgency for change of some kind. There will be no going back!

Career Change Menu

Tick the statements that apply to you.

You want to change career – anything sounds better than where you are now.	☐
You might want a change of career – if you really knew what else you could do.	☐
You hate what you are doing now.	☐
You have had a break from work (through illness, redundancy, unemployment, childbirth or childcare responsibility or something else).	☑
You never chose the job you are in – it chose you or you just fell into it.	☐
You know you are not using your full potential.	☑

continued

You really can change your life   **◄3}**

continued

You would like to find out what your full potential is.	❏
You think you are not clever because you didn't do well at school.	❏
Your job has changed and you no longer like it.	❏
You used to like your job but now you are bored.	❏
You have never really had any good, professional careers advice (the chance to talk to an expert about your personal qualities, skills, abilities and interests and how they match different careers).	❏
You really want a change but don't know where to start.	❏
You know that you don't like what you are doing now, but you are not sure what else you could do.	❏
You really don't know what else is out there and whether it would suit you better, be better or be possible for you to do.	❏
You are being forced to change career due to unemployment, downsizing, ill health, outplacement/redundancy.	❏

You might find that you have ticked quite a few of the menu options because this situation of someone needing, even yearning for a career change is more common than anyone realises; it will probably happen to everyone in their working life, at least once if not several times. Amazingly, though, for every one of the permutations in the Career Change Menu there is a real world answer, a chance for a positive life change. This book is designed to see you through all the menu options and even some not listed, so that you can feel enlightened, see a clear path and then take action to make things happen for you, so read on.

Quick answers to Career Change Menu options

Below are some general answers to common career change problems as listed in the Career Change Menu. It is useful to scan through all of them as well as looking at the ones you ticked as particularly applicable to you. For more in-depth strategies and realistic ways to deal with these problems see the relevant chapters.

You want to change career

This probably means you hate what you do or are just bored or apathetic about it. The easiest thing in this situation is to do nothing and rest miserably in the comfort zone of doing something predictable. You may feel that you are lucky to have a job, it may even pay well, or allow you to support loved ones or do interesting activities in your spare time. You may feel it is a means to an end and that it would be selfish to give it up and cause those around you to experience upheaval due to your dissatisfaction. You may believe that there is nothing better or that to go for some-thing better would involve a great financial cost or be a burden of some kind to those around you.

Try a cost/benefit analysis of this and you will see how unbalanced this thinking really is!

Costs of making a change	Benefits of making a change
It may require further study/training that might have a financial cost.	Some courses are free or have a very minimal cost, and there are ways of funding more expensive study/retraining, which can spread the cost. You have to believe that you are worth the investment of time and money. See Chapter 8.
Further study/retraining may result in less time being available for dependants etc.	If you are doing something that stimulates and interests you those around you will notice and benefit from your happier demeanour!
Once you research what might be available it may make you unhappier staying where you are.	Doing something for yourself is uplifting and life enhancing, and whatever the outcome you will benefit from the mind shift you will have set in motion that proclaims 'I am worth all this!'
There is a risk you will try something and fail.	The worst scenario is that it may not work out, but you will have developed in some way, and this in turn might take you in other, more exciting directions.

continued

continued

	In fact, research shows that the risk of failure in this kind of adventure is extremely remote if you go about it with a positive, diligent spirit.
Doing something that you dislike or that bores you has the power to erode self-esteem and encourages a cynical 'why bother' approach that has a debilitating effect in the whole of your life, but it is safe!	By harnessing the wanting, the desire for change, you take a step into the blue and introduce the possibility of something better in your life, and this first step can produce immeasurable benefits for you and those around you.
Sub-total reality = zero cost	Sub-total likelihood = endless benefits

As a real starting point you need to accept the challenge in Chapter 2 and answer the question 'Are you worth it'? Don't be tempted to skip this chapter as it is the foundation to the strategy that will ensure you can reach out and grab the brilliant future that is out there for you.

You might want a change of career – if you really knew what else you could do

There are two distinct themes to this sentence, which are fairly simple to analyse. The first is that you might want a career change. In a nutshell, 'might' is just an avoidance tactic to dodge acknowledgement of a real desire for change, a failsafe mechanism that spares you the pain and fear of recognising that you are not where you want to be. 'Might' suggests that you might be where you want to be, but are not sure. Be honest with yourself and admit that if you think 'I might want a change of career' then what you are doing probably isn't entirely right and you do want a career change. This does not have to be a major change, but it will be a shift of some kind. So for 'might' read 'want' in this sentence and you'll be closer to your real feelings on the matter!

The second part of the sentence is equally revealing: 'if you really knew what else you could do'. The subliminal message is, 'There's probably nothing else I can do', which reeks of 'Why bother?' and 'I'm not much good'. To really get beyond this kind of negative/persecution complex thinking, it is important to do some realistic self-examination and I would direct you to Chapters 2 and 3 for more help with this.

The more obvious message is that to discover the 'what else' may be beyond you or take a great deal of time and effort. In simple terms, I can only assure you of three things:

1. There is a mountain of 'what else' out there.
2. It takes very little time and effort to find out about the 'what else' factor, if you follow my advice.
3. Having found out 'what else' is available you can decide whether or not to make a change, and what type.

You hate what you are doing now

This rather miserable situation has the most amazing springboard for change within its sad scenario. By analysing in minute detail the current work you do, you can find the seeds of a new career profile hidden amongst the minutiae of your present job description. Think of yourself as a restorer of fine art who, whilst cleaning an old painting, begins to see the glimmer of another, more wonderful painting beneath the surface. The better career for you is lurking beneath the surface just like that wonderful painting, waiting to be discovered. Try an audit such as the real life scenario shown of someone who longed to make a change, but had no clues about what he could move into. You'll see that the clues are all there.

Beneath the surface audit

Job you hate – painter and decorator	Job you would like
No longer like being outdoors most of time	A job that might be mainly indoors
Too little contact with people	A job with more people contact
Very little chance for creativity	A job where imagination/problem solving/creativity could be used
Little chance to use caring nature	A job where caring skills could be used
Irregular work as self-employed person	Regular employment, possibly employed by someone else
Lack of variety	A job with a variety of different aspects and tasks
Lack of earning potential	A job with better earning potential

Suddenly a new career profile begins to emerge that points to other career options, which in this case might include more artistic or social careers. In addition, by adding in any other experience or minor good points of the present job, other alternatives might appear. In the example the painter and decorator had enjoyed working at a sheltered accommodation complex for retired people and begun to realise that he had a talent for communicating with the elderly. He decided to explore career areas such as residential social work as a way of combining his interests. Alternatively, he could have looked at occupational or art therapy where work with the elderly is common, and medical social work where work is hospital based. He also considered teaching basic life skills to handicapped adults and training to be a tutor of painting and decorating to young apprentices. These are only some of the career options he could usefully explore, but this example shows the value of looking at the negative side of your present career and then turning over to the positive side. Finding a new general career direction like this can be quite exhilarating. Simply stated, if you can find what you don't like, you have the basics of what you do like hidden beneath. Give it a try.

Job you hate Write what you hate about it	Job you would like Write the opposite of what you hate here

You may feel that you don't have the expertise to work through this process on your own, but with help from a professional careers adviser/counsellor it really would be a piece of cake, especially if you had done some of the self-analysis groundwork yourself. Sometimes it's even fun to do this with a friend. For more on careers advice see Chapter 4.

You have had a break from work

A break from work, for whatever reason, can have a devastating effect on confidence and leave you with the feeling that you have nothing to offer or that you are virtually unemployable. Sometimes the people around you collude in this negative thinking and reinforce your own ideas of how un-skilled/underqualified/inexperienced you are. Some parents, partners or friends are more comfortable with you the way you are, needing them still. Some might feel threatened by any possible success you might have, so they frighten you with warnings of failure. This is not always the case of course, but it does happen, so be strong when you encounter this sort of 'advice', and realise that this is nothing to do with your real ability or potential, but more about the insecurities of other people.

Your actual ability or potential is a totally unknown quantity, until you try something, and it is an undeniable fact that, barring a serious handi-cap, if you were able to do something once (for example, if you used to have a job), then you will be able to do something again. I call it the Cat's Cradle Law.

The Cat's Cradle Law

Remember the playground game where you wound a piece of wool round the fingers of both hands and performed various complicated manoeuvres to create patterns? You may think you've forgotten how to play, but the chances are that if you get a piece of wool and start twiddling it round your fingers you will remember – through instinct alone.

The point of course is that a career break, like a Cat's Cradle break, however long it may be, can be overcome by self-belief and having a go. It might sound silly to you but, believe me, the principle is the same, and should you find yourself despairing of ever being able to return to work due to lack of confidence, I suggest you try whispering 'Cat's Cradle' or some such nonsense as a protective mantra. More about career breaks and how to handle them in Chapter 3.

You never chose the job you are in

There is something serendipitous about the jobs we find ourselves in, that is, that we find them by chance, and sometimes they suit us quite well. Even if they do suit us, we change, jobs change or for some reason we want a change. There is no law that says we have to stay in one job till we die. It is always worth checking out what else there is. More about this in Chapter 4.

You know you are not using your full potential

There is a distinct possibility that everyone in the human race falls into this category, as even high achievers are probably not utilising every bit of their potential. However, if you have a sense that you are working on half-power, it would be interesting to see how different it would be at full power. Think of it this way – candlelight seems very romantic, but if you really want to see something clearly, you would choose electric 'full power' lighting over candles any day. Staying in the candlelight is comfortable and appealing, just like staying as you are, but stretching yourself and exploiting your potential is full power electrical energy and it is unbeatable. See Chapter 10 for unleashing your potential.

You think you are not clever because you didn't do well at school

Education can be a gift or a poison, depending on the individual experience. So many factors influence how we learn and whether we make the most of learning. Too often people are turned off learning at an early age and this causes an almost automatic negative reflex at the mere mention of education or related words. Try this game to check your response. Look down the following list of words and as you read each one put a tick or a cross according to your automatic response. Don't think too long. Just read the word and give a tick for a good feeling, a cross for a bad feeling.

Word	Tick or Cross	Word	Tick or Cross
Qualifications		Lessons	
Learning		Essay	
Teacher		Punctuation	
Maths		Spelling	

If you find you have a majority of crosses, that is bad reactions to 'bad vibe' educational words, it is probable that you fall into one, several or all of the following 'mental bruise' categories:

- School always made you feel stupid.
- You struggled with basic skills such as English and Maths.
- You were fine at primary school but found secondary school daunting.
- You left school with low qualifications.
- You found exams and tests difficult.
- You were not engaged by school and learning – it did not enthral you.
- You were not motivated at school.
- You messed around at school or other people messed around and distracted you.
- You started off well but lost interest.
- Outside factors stopped you from working, like family problems, illness, moving around a lot.

These mental bruises can be more long lasting and life threatening than the physical kind. Quite often people survive with a myriad of these bruises and are unaware of them, until they realise they want something more from their life and find that these past experiences of education are around, ready to trip them up at every opportunity. For some people the mere thought of a return to education, either as a way of improving employment prospects or of developing new skills, is enough to cause a mental clampdown and a resultant backing away from anything that involves learning. This defensive reaction is a learned one against the pain of remembered failure.

However, invariably, it is not only bad experiences of learning that are committed to memory. In fact everything we do, from brushing our teeth to smiling, is a learned response, and many other types of learning have a successful outcome, but we often only choose to remember the unsuccessful learning. For most of us the greater part of our learning is successful, but mental bruise victims need to focus on their good learning rather than the bad, to expel the learning ghosts of the past. Most can remember something they were good at in school or a time when things went well. Getting the right kind of support for learning and choosing the right method to suit you now is the best way forward, for healing those bruises, banishing those ghosts and making miracles happen.

It is worth considering the difference in focus and learning styles of young people and adult learners to clarify why a return to learning and life-long learning can be successful and should be your goal.

A light-hearted comparison of learning style/motivation

Typical young learner	Typical adult learner
Influenced by friends/peers	Influenced by unwillingness to be stuck in rut
Interested in football/fun	Interested in self-development
Motivated by money/fear of being told off	Motivated by enthusiasm for change and for study
Focused on self-interest	Focused/committed to maximise learning opportunity
Resistant to formal learning	Ready to submit to formal/informal learning

It's easy to see why, once adults opt for a return to learning, they can push themselves beyond their expectations, due solely to the desire to do it for themselves. Never underestimate the power of self-motivation.

And finally, all the government predictions for the future of work hinge on the need for a continuous learning culture in this country, and that means that you, me, the butcher, baker and candlestick maker have to be committed to investing in ourselves to the extent that we constantly update our skills, keep up with the pace of change and look for ways to sharpen our competitive edge. The government calls this lifelong learning, and to protect yourself from the slings and arrows of the 21st century's outrageous fortune, you need to sign up for this wholeheartedly. It's the only insurance worth having: learning keeps you earning.

Your job has changed and you no longer like it/ You used to like your job but are bored

These two are very common, and simple to deal with swiftly. First, it is a fact of working life today that jobs change, develop, become defunct, so don't be surprised by this. If the job changes it may be that you resist these changes and become less interested in it, because it is no longer comfortable or because, deep down, it is making you feel insecure. This could be a sign to you to 'upskill', an ugly word but a necessary process in a fast moving employment situation, where technology demands higher skill levels. Through the 'thrill' of upskilling/retraining you may find a new interest in your job or that better promotion opportunities arise. It is likely that most employees are either being forced kicking and screaming, or throwing themselves willingly, into higher levels of computer literacy than they had anticipated, but along with numeracy and literacy this is a key skill that cannot be avoided.

If your job has changed out of all recognition and you feel that your interest level in it is zero then it is time for a change, but resist the impulse to jump at anything. It is still worth going about a change of career direction in a measured way. See Chapter 4 for this. Boredom in a job is a sure sign that you are wasting your potential and are ready for a new challenge. Again, take some time to discover what you don't like about your present situation so that you can assess what it is you do want. Again Chapter 4 will help with this.

You have never really had any good, professional careers advice

Most people can benefit from this and there are many sources of help, either free of charge or at a minimal cost. Details can be found in Chapter 9.

You really want a change but don't know where to start

This statement is the main reason that many people do nothing and the real reason for this book. If you read this book you will not be able to use this excuse, because every eventuality is covered, including how and where to start. The great thing is that there are so many options available; often finding out what's out there is the easy part, deciding which one to choose is harder. But don't even worry about deciding, because help is at hand for that, too! See Chapter 4 and 5.

You know that you don't like what you are doing now, but you are not sure what else you could do

There is a fear within most of us that we are capable of doing only one thing and we have to stick with it or risk losing everything. But many human beings have an enormous untapped capacity and, once you have explored your full potential, you will know all the amazing things you can do as alternatives to what you are doing now. See Chapter 4.

You really don't know what else is out there

This is the 'what else' and 'what's out there' fear again. There is always something else out there and there are always ways for you to seek out what will fit with your individual situation, however complex it seems. See Chapter 4 for all you need to know about this.

You are being forced to change career

Forced career change of any kind brings a mixture of resentment, fear and mental bruises, which can worsen a potentially bad situation. Invariably, though, despite all the negative elements of these situations, they can result in the most life-enhancing changes if positive, resourceful attitudes are cultivated. See especially Chapters 3 and 6.

Those are some quick answers to the Career Change Menu. I hope, by now, you are beginning to realise that so much more is possible than you imagined, and only the willingness to explore your choices is needed. Work no longer has to be a dirty word, something to be endured until retirement. The Dickensian workhouse mentality still exists, but you don't need to subscribe to it. You have nothing to lose by trying out possible futures for size – it just requires an imaginative leap.

CHAPTER 2 | Are you worth it?

Most people would answer the question 'Am I worth it?' with 'Of course I am!' but, invariably, people say this and then act differently. They put their own needs or dreams in second place to others, out of self-lessness or because, deep down, they might think that others are worthier. But you are worthy!

You'll be tempted to skip this chapter, possibly because no one likes too much self-analysis. You may think that you just want to cut to the 'How do I make a change bit?' with its clear guidelines. The problem is that skipping the self-examination is something like finding yourself in a maze with a blindfold on. On its own the maze is tricky enough and you wish you had a map or even a bird's-eye view; but blindfolded you can't see the maze and you can't see yourself and so you could stumble around forever, without hope of finding a path, let alone an exit. Lack of self-knowledge is like rotting away in the maze with the blindfold on. At first taking the blind-fold off is difficult, and you may even replace it by peeping through your fingers, but eventually you'll see yourself in the full light of day as the unique human being you are; you'll even see the maze better!

So, you need to put aside some quality time to do this and you have to start by believing you're worth the effort. I'm going to suggest a few exer-cises – some may work better than others for you, but they all work by peel-ing away the layers to find the real 'you'. They take some mental work, and can be done in privacy or sometimes with a close friend. They can be fun! To check out your feelings of self-worth, try the internal language test or how your head talks!

Head talking

Over the period of a week, make a note of what internal conversations you have with yourself. Keep a small notebook and when you are working, about to fall asleep, exercising or in conversation with someone, become aware of what your head is saying. Typically, you may find yourself driving to work and imagining calamitous encounters or thinking ahead to various catastrophic scenarios; you may be saying to yourself 'I'll probably not do that report on time' or 'My boss seems to think I'm not up to more responsibility'.

Make sure that you write down all these random thoughts, good or bad, throughout the whole week. At the end of the week do a quick analysis; it's likely that much of your internal language is negative. If there is some good, positive language, highlight it, as these may point you towards real desires and needs in your life; for example, if you had written 'I wonder if I could contact x about more training in y', it is more than likely a sound impulse that you should follow.

Negative thinking is a bad habit we all fall into, based on a number of things, including fear of failure, being ground down by difficult circumstances, lack of appreciation and unnurtured self-belief. We all need to eliminate this unbalanced thinking because it is a burden on our thinking space. It is a waste of space. Resolve to practise positive thinking instead and choose to ignore or zap any of these unhelpful, wayward thoughts. These kinds of thoughts are meaningless with regard to the future you want.

Imagine your thinking space as the memory on a computer; sometimes you have loads of rubbish that you need to delete, at other times you need to make a note not to 'save' useless stuff – negative thinking is just useless stuff you saved by mistake. Now you need to learn how to delete the rubbish and decide not to save the useless stuff any more. It is possible; you just need to want to do it.

Deleting the rubbish

The trick is to first identify the rubbish. The trouble is that you're quite attached to it and it's attached to you. It may even look like a rather pretty weed, but it's still a weed. Here are some examples of weeds that desperate career changers have presented me with:

1. **The 'too old' weed**
   'I may be too old to learn a new skill.'
2. **The 'I may not cope' weed**
   'It may be too hard to go for a more demanding job. I might be better sticking where I am.'
3. **The 'bad parent' weed**
   'I can't go for anything better or my children might suffer.'
4. **The 'frying pan/fire' weed**
   'I don't want to risk going for something else. It may not work out.'
5. **The 'nothing better' weed**
   'There's probably nothing else I can do.'

The fact is that there is some genuine justification for all these weeds, but this is not reason enough for abandoning real needs. Needs can beat weeds any day! Each one of these weeds is poisonous and their antidotes can be swiftly administered, as follows.

1. 'Too old'

No one is too old. Just look at the explosion of mature students studying courses as diverse as computing, law, boatbuilding, gamekeeping, patchwork, homeopathy – the list is endless. We only stop learning when we die.

2. 'I may not cope'

The wish for something more demanding is proof itself that someone has untapped potential. Mental or physical stretching is exhilarating and you can build up 'fitness' in stages – see Chapter 4.

3. 'Bad parent'

We all have responsibilities and commitments that can weigh us down, but children especially are very adaptable and they won't suffer by having a happy, fulfilled parent. They are more likely to suffer through a sad, self-sacrificing parent.

4. 'Frying pan/fire'

You cannot eliminate risk in your life. The safest job can be subject to redundancy or changing work practices. Staying put can be dangerous, too. Equipping yourself with the best package of skills, training and experience and exploiting your full potential is the least risky thing you can do and can help you deal with any eventuality.

5. 'Nothing better'

This is the common cop-out, and simply cannot compete with the facts, which are, firstly, that there are endless 'something betters' out there, as multiple careers are the future for all of us and single job lives (a job for life) are part of the past; and, secondly, that people 'can do' many things, given the chance.

And so finally in this exercise you need to take some time to identify and delete the rubbish and misinformed assumptions that are holding you back. Start with a list of 'Reasons why I hesitate' and the 'Antidotes'; an example of which is shown.

Reasons why I hesitate to try an evening course in counselling

Reason	Antidote
Getting to know strange people	They could be interesting
Writing essays	I'll ask for help
Going to college after a day's work	I'll be tired but it will be stimulating
What if I hate it?	So what? It's only a 16-week course. I'm bound to learn something
What if I find it tough?	I'll get help and it will stretch me

Now fill in your own 'Reasons why I hesitate' grid; it's the best way to delete the rubbish and build yourself up at the same time.

Reason for not doing...	Antidote

Try doing this whenever you come up with an objection for doing something, and you will find after a while, that you do it automatically, and that eventually you are out of the habit of saving the rubbish. Just think how much space you will be freeing up for plans and strategies to get you where you want to be!

Now we need to move on to some self-nurturing; this is a bit like pruning a rather overgrown plant. You're the plant. You're all over the place and looking a little bedraggled. We've started by cutting off all the dead wood (deleting the rubbish) and now you're looking a little small and bare but really tidy. Have you got this picture? We need to start by feeding you a bit and keeping the bugs of negative thinking and self-destruct at bay, so you can grow into a strong and vigorous plant. This requires self-discipline and the need to be constantly vigilant, but you just have to practise new habits of positive awareness and self-coaching. See later for re-laxation and cognitive rehearsal techniques and Chapter 10 for self-coaching.

Feeding and nurturing comes next and we can call these the ego stroking exercises.

Ego stroking – 1

For most of us, memories of things going wrong come easily to mind, but the times of personal achievements seem harder to remember. Within your personal achievements, however small, are the seeds of self-knowledge about your abilities, skills and potential. These are the clues you need to create a fully fleshed-out picture of yourself, so over a seven-day period, take ten minutes a day, and give yourself the following task: think over your past and present, and each day come up with a memory of a moment when you knew you had done something well. Your first reaction may be that you cannot think of anything but, with time, you will remember moments of value in your life, even perhaps most insignificant things. I'll give you an example to help you get the idea.

Example of moments of value

Day	Moment	What it means about me
Monday	Recalled Dad praising me for coming 23rd in a cross-country of 200 kids!	I can be determined and can do things on my own.
Tuesday	Today someone asked for my help with writing a letter of complaint.	I can sometimes use words well and like to help.
Wednesday	I visited a blind old lady every week for two years when I was at school.	I can be responsible and committed.

continued

continued

Thursday	I had a main part once in a play at school.	I used to be less self-conscious than I am now.
Friday	I organised a petition to the local council for a safe play area.	I care about the community.
Saturday	I made a patchwork cot cover by hand.	I have good practical skills.
Sunday	I once got 13% in Chemistry but it just made me laugh!	I can bounce back from failure.

Now you try this exercise, and resist the impulse to give up. Be persistent and spend the ten minutes each day to recall these moments of value. Look at the analysis at the end of the week – the 'What it means about me' column – and you will have the beginning of a profile about yourself that should also give you ideas of some of your key strengths that will act as ego stroking. The strange thing is that we often offer ego stroking to those we love, but forget to do it for ourselves!

Your moments of value

Day	Moment	What it means about me
Monday		
Tuesday		
Wednesday		
Thursday		
Friday		
Saturday		
Sunday		

Once you've tried this you are part-way through a self-revelatory process that will help you know what it is you are working with when you embark on your career change plan. I used images of a map, a maze and a blindfold before; now you're peeking through your hands. It's worth mentioning that when I speak of maps there is good news and bad news. The good news is that there is a map that can help you see your way through the maze of possibilities, but the bad news is that you have to create it yourself, and it is made up of everything about you balanced against everything that is available to you. Once you have created this map you will be in a position to make decisions and plans.

Ego stroking – 2

The 'you' that is you is made up of an infinitesimal number of parts, but the parts that are useful for your career planning fall into the following categories; personality characteristics/qualities or temperament, skills/abilities/experience and interests. We need to uncover the details of these three areas to make a meaningful map of who you are. Set yourself a little project, again over about a week, to find yourself. Use the chart below as a guide and mentally tell yourself to brainstorm words and phrases that fit you over the course of a week. Have the chart close at hand, and whenever a word or phrase comes to mind write it down in the relevant box. As you go through the day make a mental note of personality characteristics and skills/abilities that you observe or become aware of. Consider what characteristics you display typically in a work environment or through your interests. At the end of the week review your chart and you will begin to see the 'You' map. It ought to be quite flattering and positive. You should also be able to identify something unique about yourself; this will probably be the strongest characteristic.

Categories	Random words/phrases that come into my mind through the week
Personality qualities/ temperament eg quiet, kind, hardworking, sociable, friendly	

continued

continued

Skills eg communication, numeracy, team work, organisational	
Abilities eg an ability at Biology or ability to listen well or to lead others	
Experience eg types of work or life experiences and what these have developed in me	
Interests eg anything you love to do	
Only do this at the end of the week What is unique about me and transferable skills (see next section for help with this)	

If you were able to do this with a close friend or someone who knows you well, you could ask them to add their input to any of the categories. You could even swap charts and help each other!

Transferable skills – the extra ingredient

You might have uncovered these while completing your chart, but just to ensure we have not missed anything it is worth focusing on them before we move on. Whatever you have been doing all your life you have been using skills, some perhaps you were born with, some you have developed through any and every life experience, good or bad. Even a bad experience can have a positive outcome for you. Here are some examples.

John worked as a traffic warden, a job he hated. He gained experience and developed skills in staying calm in the face of abuse, working under pressure and organising his time.

Transferable skills: organisational/time management/working under pressure

Ben liked his job and had to deal with overseas customers by email. He once used a French greeting to a French customer and she was so pleased that it encouraged him to start a French conversation class to improve his schoolboy French. He followed this with Dutch, then Spanish. He became the highest rated customer service adviser.

Transferable skills: customer service and language skills

Sam was computerphobic, but in his first job there was a computer on his desk and he just had to have a go. He proved to himself that he could learn this new skill, despite a tricky start.

Transferable skills: willing to learn and IT (information technology) skills

Josh worked in a fast food restaurant and found he hated cooking, but was given food hygiene training, which tempted him to look at environmental health as a career.

Transferable skills: food hygiene/scientific skills

Hannah did some voluntary work with a vacation playscheme for young children; she found this helped her develop good listening skills and patience.

Transferable skills: listening skills and patience

Jack had always done a milk round for a local farmer; he found that he liked an outdoor job and could cope with the early morning starts.

Transferable skills: reliability/practicality/being able to wake up early

So be sure that you have not missed these aspects of your life experience and that they are shown on your chart in some shape or form.

Map reading

With some diligence, you should have produced a fine 'You' map and be ready for your next steps, which involve plotting your course. However, if you found the last exercise difficult and still feel as if you have no clue about yourself, then it may help to see a professional careers adviser or occupational psychologist, who can go through this process of self-exploration with you, helping you to uncover what you have to offer. See Chapter 4 for details of this.

With your completed chart, you have the clues to possible career directions that you can take, but you have to look carefully at what you have uncovered about yourself and first brainstorm job titles that may fit with your personal profile as detailed on the chart. If, as is likely, two or three jobs come to mind as a result of this analysis, you will need to score them as to how well they seem to match you. If they all score quite well, then they are all worth researching, and this is covered in Chapter 4. If one career seems to fit you better than others, look into that first.

If no clear ideas of jobs come to mind, don't despair – it just means that you need to do some 'what's out there' checking first. Save your map/chart and you can use it again in Chapter 4. If, by the end of Chapter 4, you still have no clue what to do then, again, see a professional adviser or occupational psychologist, as detailed in Chapter 4.

'I wonder if' career ideas

As a careers adviser, I often find that my clients have a career idea that I call an 'I wonder if'. With some probing they might say:

> *'I wonder if I'm good enough to train to be a graphic designer?'*

> *'I've always wondered if I could be a psychologist?'*

> *'I've always wondered what a mediator does?'*

Sometimes they mention it right away but at other times I have to uncover it by direct or indirect questioning. Sometimes clients feel embarrassed to mention it or feel that it would reveal some unusually 'great expectation' or some unattainable goal, especially if they are modest or unassuming. Often, as I am floundering around and trying to get to grips with what they really want, I just say, 'Give me any ideas of careers that interest you, however wild or unattainable they may seem to you; everyone has an "I wonder if" career.' Invariably this type of career idea can be usefully researched and can also be the source of related career ideas; for example, someone who had an 'I wonder if' about counselling might also look into advocacy, mediation and mentoring.

If you have an 'I wonder if' career in mind, check this against your map/chart in the following way.

I wonder if I could be an interior designer?	Map/chart clues
Guess list of what might be needed	
Friendly character – self-employment or contractual work is often part of this job	Can work on own/sociable
Strong imagination/creativity required	Creative/artistic skills
Great talent needed	Artistic talent – unique ability
Passion for fabrics/carpets/curtains/lighting required	Interest in textiles/colours/lighting
Business promotion	Business minded
Matching score	100% match or ten out of ten

Giving yourself a score out of ten is a great way to analyse how suited you are to a career, in your own estimate, but you would still need to research the career area fully before making a final decision. Full research and decision making is covered in Chapter 5.

Now try this yourself.

I wonder if I could be (career/job name)?	Map/chart clues from Ego stroking 2
Write guess list of what might be needed	
Matching score	

So we come to the last part of this self-knowledge trip, and you should be beginning to have a really good map. To complete it we need to do a bit of colouring in/shading and defining features. To do this, and to make your map unique, we have to deal with your needs and wants. Most people seeking a change of career start by stating what they want. Some people need help with this. Start by formulating a really clear 'want' statement. It is what you want to be. Large companies often call this their 'mission statement'. Typical 'want' or personal mission statements might be:

'I want to return to work after a break but I no longer want to be in business. I want something caring.'

The self-discovery and 'what's out there' process can clarify this statement to:

'I want a change of career to a caring profession in the medical field. I am looking into the therapies, such as radiotherapy and speech therapy.'

Another 'want' statement might be:

'I want a more fulfilling job that uses my sporting interest and interest in young people. I'm looking at PE teaching, coaching and youth work.'

'Need' statements are connected to the particular circumstances of someone's life, such as financial security or independence, dependants, or limitations due to disabilities or health problems or geographical constraints. 'Needs' statements are similar to a company's 'vision statement' and are about where you want to go, according to the circumstances of your life. Typical 'need' statements are:

'I need to be earning enough money to come off state benefits.'

'I need to make a difference to someone's life.'

'I need to work within travelling distance of X.'

'I need a job where I can be sitting down due to my arthritis.'

Obviously there will be some overlap between your wants and needs, but it is still worth spending time to clarify what it is exactly that you want and need. Try this last exercise as a way of giving yourself some first action points in your career planning strategy.

I don't know what I want but...

Here's an example of a real life 'wants and needs' manifesto.

I don't know what I want but...	First steps I can take
I want a job using Human Biology	Research jobs with Biology
I want to help people	Look into hospital jobs with Biology
I need to work locally	Phone hospital Personnel Department
I might need to work part time	Check local newspapers for typical part-time jobs
I want a practical job	Look into medical and industrial laboratory jobs

Doing this means that you decide your criteria for the future you want. Notice how you need to make a small research project out of each want or need.

Here's a second example. This is for someone with a longing for education, but no clear idea where this could take him or her, and a need to keep on supporting a family while studying.

I don't know what I want but...	First steps I can take
I want to go to university locally	Contact local universities for prospectuses
I need to get some better qualifications	Find out what qualifications I will need to gain a university place
I need to carry on working while studying	Find out from local colleges about evening/weekend study
I need a professional career with good earning potential	Research university courses locally that lead into professional careers; contact professional bodies to find out typical salary levels

Your own wants and needs manifesto will be different but will set you on your way in a clear and specific manner. Give it a try.

I don't know what I want but...	First steps I can take

And finally, the most important key to getting where you want to be or discovering your true potential is you and:

- what you are prepared to do
- how far you are prepared to go
- how much discomfort you may be prepared to put up with.

If your life doesn't change it won't be your circumstances or lack of chances that are to blame; it will be your motivation for career change that is weak. You really have to want it enough and follow through with your plans. Don't get hijacked along the way or be put off from starting by fear of the unknown. Just take the first step, and the thrill of starting on your own path will buoy you up to the next step.

CHAPTER 3

What's stopping you starting?

If you are brimming with confidence and feel your self-esteem is at an optimum level then you may not need this chapter; but as the reason for seeking a career change is often that a present situation is wrong, usually some denting of self-confidence has gone on too. Launching into the career search process with even a slightly bruised attitude will end in failure and more dents to your confidence. A brief but thorough self-confidence building programme is therefore advised, and this is what this chapter will cover. You don't need to be a gibbering wreck to benefit from this, as even those with a fairly robust self-esteem have blips of self-doubt. These can cause problems if not handled well.

There are some common factors that seem to create low self-confidence, typified by the following comments:

'I've not worked for six years while I brought up our children. I'm ready to return to work but need a term-time only job of about 15 hours a week — and I can't think what I can do. I'm not sure I know how to get a job any more. Things have changed. I have no experience.'

'I have been unemployed for a while. I only have experience of low-paid jobs. I have no qualifications. There's just nothing I can do.'

'I have been ill and my health problems mean I can only work part time. I need to retrain, but don't know what would suit me.'

'I have recently been made redundant from engineering. I no longer want to do this, but am not trained for anything else.'

'I never did well at school. What can I do?'

Let's look in some detail at these factors.

Parenting break

Let's begin with 'I've not worked for five years'; of course, only paid work has value! Parenting, with its diversity of skills and demands, is seen here as a low-skilled occupation. A change of mindset is first required to view it in a more realistic light, with its transferable skills of caring, communicating, listening, organising, working under pressure etc. What could someone with these skills do? Just about anything!

Secondly, the restrictions of dependant children seem overwhelming, but there are term-time only jobs and part-time jobs – see examples of this in Chapter 6. Thirdly, it is correct to say the job market has changed and different tactics are required, but this will not be a problem for someone with the flexibility gained from caring for young children.

Finally, the 'no experience' statement is simply inaccurate, for the same reasons as before. Parenting gives a multitude of experiences that can be used in a wide range of jobs and would be marketable to many employers.

Obviously this type of break needs to be viewed in a new light, as a fertile ground for skills and experiences, which can direct someone to the next stage of their career path. It is not a wasted experience as long as it can be purged of negative overtones. It is quite natural, though, to feel this way, but the thought, when it comes to mind, needs to be swatted like an irritating fly, then followed by a confidence building skills audit to clarify things, see page 37.

Unemployment break

This is one of life's trials that many of us will experience. It is easy to come up with trite answers to this, but although everyone should be employable, there are some people who are unemployable for a number of reasons. Obviously, severe ill health or disabilities may make it extremely difficult for someone to gain employment. However, some people actually make themselves unemployable through personal attitude and lack of self-awareness. Add to that the process of unemployment, which knocks at a person's self-esteem, and an unemployment break begins to look like a life sentence.

Having experienced unemployment myself, and having worked to help unemployed young people and adults gain work successfully, I can only suggest things that have worked (see the list below), and stress again that *it is just a break*. Keeping a sound perspective is vital, and refusing to succumb to depression and cynicism is crucial.

Things that work

1. Know what you have to offer – write it down – try the confidence building skills audit on page 37.
2. Know what you really want (main plan) and what you will be prepared to consider (back-up plan).
3. Devise a strategy with clear steps that you can take to achieve your goal.
4. Create a structure to your day that involves working through action steps, finding and following employment leads.
5. Tell everyone you are looking for work – use your network of contacts in every aspect of your life.
6. Check all sources of employment leads, including newspapers, journals, recruitment agencies, past colleagues, job centres/careers centres, the Internet.
7. Use voluntary work to gain new skills, update experience and as a 'lead in' to paid work.
8. Go for a 'good enough' job if it holds promise of better things.
9. Work on your personal development through confidence building tricks, college courses (which are free to unemployed people), internal dialogue/positive thinking etc.
10. Use the best tools – a great CV and job search strategy, a good attitude and persistence.

Redundancy or outplacement break

Similar to a straightforward unemployment break but with its own particular set of problems, this can cause the worst kind of self-confidence dent. However the redundancy process is handled by the employer, invariably those being outplaced feel bruised, regardless of how happy or miserable life was working for that employer. It is worth looking at research on those selected for redundancy, which shows that typically they are resourceful, individualistic, hard-working characters rather than the bottom of the pile employees. Nonetheless, redundancy means a new start in an employment market that might be very unfamiliar, so a good positive employment strategy is advisable, see 'Things that Work' list. In my redundancy/outplacement counselling experience, these are the key things I have found that help.

Things that work

1. Usually there is some lead-in time to an announcement of a redundancy, with further time for working out notice; this can be used to update

skills through Training and Enterprise Council (TEC)-funded training (see Chapter 9) or short courses available through the appropriate trade union or local colleges. Some companies have an arrangement for free courses of this kind. Often the most useful course is some kind of update or even a beginners computing course; it will be a good CV item, even if it only says 'Currently studying for City & Guilds Information Technology course covering spreadsheets and the Internet' and you started it a week before!

2. Use the lead-in/notice time to make a list of business contacts outside the company and start contacting them immediately about possible work opportunities – these might be part time, temporary or consultancy based. Consider all offers carefully.

3. Use the lead-in/notice time to 'network' with colleagues within the company and at other company sites for possible alternative employment.

4. Work out what your financial situation will be and take good advice. You need to know whether you will be able to afford full-time retraining before taking a new job or whether you will need to get a job quickly. You may look at an early retirement scenario and also need to look at other work options like self-employment, contractual, part-time or voluntary work, or you may choose to cultivate hobbies or interests.

5. Start with your own self-assessment and confidence building skills audit to work out your strengths, your selling points and what you have to offer.

6. Start checking out 'what's out there' (see Chapters 4/5). This might involve a complete change or self-employment.

7. Create one, two or three brilliant CVs, aimed at different work opportunities, and use them in a targeted employment strategy, which means discovering which employers you want to work for and the best way to approach them. It might mean sending CVs off to contacts you have made in that company or using your networking to gain contacts who will recommend you.

8. Give yourself a target of contacting at least one employment lead per day, preferably in person, and make sure other people are out there contacting people for you, too.

9. Check professional journals, local newspaper employment pages and register with good recruitment agencies – check these on the Internet.

10. Use the Internet for research, making contacts and effective job seeking – there are some very good job search sites, see Chapter 10.

Health and other restrictions on your work choices

These are facts of life but it is a mistake to get them out of perspective. It is likely that a large number of people have restrictions on their work choices, which they have to work around. The following are typical and encompass most of us.

'I need to work/train/study within travelling distance of X'

Most people have this kind of locational restriction, so the main way to deal with it is to accept it, if it is real, and look for work/training or career changing options within that defined geographical area. But let's check if it is real first. Some employers/colleges/training centres may offer free or sub-sidised transport and shared transport may also be available. Public transport may be possible, especially with railcards/buscards etc.

It may be possible to be a 'remote' worker if you have access to a computer and email; this is becoming a very real option in many different career areas and is sometimes called teleworking or simply working from home. Some companies who have invested in 'hot desking' encourage employees to come into work possibly only once a week, share a desk station on that day and work from home for the rest of the time. It may be worth using a proactive approach and selling yourself to an employer for this kind of work – see Chapter 5.

It is also worth looking into the possibility of open learning/distance learning as a way of gaining new qualifications while studying at home. Although this requires great motivation, it can be a very effective way of pre-paring for a return to work by updating qualifications and skills. The sheer diversity of courses and qualifications available through this method of study is both mindblowing and fascinating, so do not overlook this potential for changing your career options by changing 'you' and what you have to offer. For a look at this interesting area, see Chapter 5.

Finally, childcare provision is a major government priority and there is a growth in pre-school and after school playclubs that can make it possible for parents to juggle work or study obligations, so this is worth investigating. Local TECs can often be a source of information on these playclubs and on 'Return to work' courses (see Chapter 9).

'I can only look for term-time work due to my children's school times'

I have done considerable research into this as it affected me personally, and can say with conviction that there are more termtime opportunities than most people realise. This is covered in depth in Chapter 6. Again, it is worth being proactive on this one and actually asking for a term-time only contract. Believe me it can work – see 'Asking for it' in Chapter 6.

'I can only work part-time due to a health problem'

This can be tricky because a health problem can be anything from slight asthma to a severe disability. Initially, a confidence building skills audit is still useful, but it needs a more focused 'What I can actually do' approach; analysing this rather than 'What I can't do' is generally more productive. With slight health problems, you could usefully target 'good' employers and see whether the problems could be overcome. Identifying these good employers may seem a bit of a minefield but this is covered in Chapter 6.

For more serious health restrictions or disabilities, say if you are wheelchair bound, it is worth contacting the disability employment adviser at local job centres, who can refer you for something called occupational assessment that will help identify what you do best; they can also offer advice on disability friendly employers. Of course you could also be looking for work at home, where the ability to travel to and fro is immaterial.

Finally, there is a proliferation in part-time work opportunities, which can be anything from 5 to 30 hours a week, so be persistent and there should be something for you. Don't forget to consider job sharing as a possible option; many employers advertise job share vacancies or are willing to consider a job sharing arrangement. Again, being proactive and selling this idea to a prospective employer can work, so see Chapter 6, 'Asking for it'.

'I need work that I can do from home'

There are many options here and these are also covered in Chapter 6. Self-discipline and motivation are needed if you want to make this work for you, but government forecasts for the future of work in the new century predict that about 40 per cent of workers will be self-employed, including Internet-related working and home-based working. Even so, the figure for home-based working of some kind is currently about 20/30 per cent, so you could be one of those workers.

'I need some training but can't afford the time or cost of further study'

Time is at a premium for all of us and the demands of a young family or caring for family members can leave little personal 'quality time', but timing, not time, is the key to this problem. Optimising your time by fitting in training alongside other aspects of your life can work, but needs careful planning. Construct an action plan that starts preparing for a career change or a return to work in small steps, each having a minimal time demand but building up to achieve your goal. Deciding on the best time for starting this is crucial as, for example, an evening course embarked upon at a busy or overloaded personal time can be a waste of time/money/effort and can result in a plummet in self-confidence.

Here are a couple of typical scenarios.

CASE STUDY: BAD TIMING

Sue's son was due to start senior school and she felt she would like to do the degree course she had always longed to do. She had not studied for 15 years but did not want to delay any longer. However, her son had problems settling down at school and needed a lot of help getting used to homework. Her degree work on a full-time basis was a heavy load and Sue felt constantly stressed by her responsibilities and her yearning to study and do well. Sue would have done better to anticipate settling-in problems for her son and herself; a better option for her might have been a foundation-style course (a degree preparation course) on a part-time basis to ease her into this higher level study. See Chapter 5 for more about this.

CASE STUDY: GOOD TIMING

Jack had been a single parent at home for three years but his daughter was due to start at a nursery five mornings a week. He wanted to build up qualifications for a return to paid work in three to four years and so looked into open learning options for the first year of his daughter's nursery schooling. He started two GCSE courses by flexible study at home through a local college and was able to fit this around the start and finish times of the nursery, but it also maximised his free times in the mornings.

Finally, the cost of study or training can deter the most motivated person, but it is worth emphasising the following:
- For those in receipt of certain benefits, such as Job Seekers Allowance, Family Credit, Income Support, Incapacity Benefit, most daytime 15/16 hour per week Access courses and evening and weekend courses are free of charge.

- Colleges often offer staged payments to spread the cost.
- Many courses for 'career returners', the unemployed or those with disabilities, run by colleges or TEC-funded training centres, are free of charge.
- There is some help with funding for study, see Chapter 8.

'I can't afford to give up my job to train for a new career'

No one has to give up a job to retrain, as there are a multitude of different ways to retrain these days – these are covered in Chapter 6. The best way to train for a new career is to develop yourself through your present job. This might mean taking any training that is offered that might be transferable to your new career direction or persuading your current employer to invest in your training so that better options within that employment emerge. You could also start in a small or major way (depending on your preferred timescale) to update your skills/qualifications through distance learning/ evening or weekend study.

'I need an earning potential of £X to support my family'

This requires some careful research, as there is nothing worse than retraining for a new career and then finding that it does not fit your financial expectations. A useful source of current salary guidelines, as well as a large range of up-to-date careers information, is a book called *Occupations* produced by the Careers and Occupational Information Centre (COIC) and found in most public careers centres/offices and good libraries. Careers advisers can also help with local knowledge of salary scales for different employers.

'I can't earn more than £X or I will lose my entitlement to benefits'

The same answer as above applies to this, but remember that the need not to earn vast amounts of money can free you to do interesting but unpaid or low-paid work – see Chapter 6.

I have tried to give some useful answers to these problems but must emphasise first that these restrictions are common rather than unusual and there are almost always ways round them; unfortunately, without help, advice and some determination, it can sometimes seem hard to discover the best solutions. What you need to know, in essence, is that there is more 'out there' than you ever imagined. More detailed advice on how to actually work round personal restrictions can be found in later chapters, including real life examples for you to follow. This section is just to rid you of the fixed belief that nothing will work out and persuade you to investigate the real possibilities of meaningful work choices, despite any personal and individual restrictions. Now you have no excuses, so go on and jump start your life!

Confidence building skills audit

A confidence building skills audit is just another way of examining what you have and where you are now – your starting point. Before doing this it is useful to do a very silly sum of how much time you have been alive/breathing/learning/experiencing. Mine would look something like this:

45 years living × 365 days = 16,225 days of skills/abilities/interests

Now do yours. Multiply the years of your life by 365. Then the next time someone asks you (or you ask yourself) what you have to offer and you feel tempted to say 'Nothing special', just think about all those days filled with every kind of experience. How could that sum work out at zero? So move into this skills audit filled with optimism rather than a weary expectation of nothing!

Allocate some time to completing the following chart with key points of your experience, broken down into clear, work-related skills, possible transferable skills and natural skills (ones you were born with or developed early on). Start in the past and move steadily forward to the present, looking at all the stages of your life so far, in intense detail, searching for clues of your uniqueness.

Lifetime	Skills audit
Pre-school Memories of things you were good at or liked to do	
Primary school Memories of strengths/abilities/interests	
Senior school As above	
Work-related What skills you have developed and used	

continued

continued

Unpaid work/voluntary work Career break time Interests and hobbies Skills gained/developed through these	

An example of a completed skills audit might help you to see the value of the exercise.

Lifetime	**Skills audit for Catherine**
Pre-school Memories of things you were good at or liked to do	Digging in the mud in the garden/examining bugs Helping to plant seeds Showing off by singing to relatives Analytical and performing skills
Primary school Memories of strengths/abilities/interests	Good at science Good at acting Interested in how things work Scientific/problem solving skills
Senior school As above	Good at science, maths and drama Made friends easily Good at explaining things to other people Interpersonal/social/communicating skills
Work-related What skills you have developed and used	First job – laboratory work in hospital Second job – haematology research and teaching medical students Third job after career break – working as a school lab assistant Scientific/training skills
Unpaid work/voluntary work and *Career break time*	Bringing up young daughter Organisational/communication/flexibility
Interests and Hobbies Skills gained/developed through these	Golf/gardening/socialising/amateur dramatics Social/outdoor/performing/people skills

Try and annotate your skills audit chart as shown in the box to focus on your key skills. Ideally, you should be framing your career plan and future career options around the skills you uncover in this audit. Your future and present career aspirations should very clearly match your individual skills package – see later chapters for more about this.

Pitfalls

A career change won't just fall into place by magic, though. Any number of things can happen to trip you up but, with that robust self-esteem we have been fostering, you should be able to remember that you are worth the effort, are ready for pitfalls and can find ways round them, and be flexible enough to change course when necessary. Here are some common pitfalls and their possible solutions.

CASE STUDY: 'TAKING ANYTHING'
Tony hated his job in an office and had always wanted to work in sport/fitness or leisure centres at a management level. He knew he needed some on-the-ground experience but couldn't afford the drop in salary this might mean. He was offered some weekend casual work at a leisure centre but refused this because he felt he could not cope with two jobs.

SOLUTION
He was advised to take some night school qualifications in coaching, fitness training and business; he did this over two years. He was offered weekend work as a fitness instructor by his fitness teacher, which he developed over the next year into a full-time career, managing and running a local gym. This worked for Tony because he took it at his own pace and it fitted with his own financial situation.

CASE STUDY: 'TAKING THE FIRST THING THAT COMES ALONG'
Mary wanted to return to work but needed a term-time only working arrangement. She went for a job at a college library that provided this but had a very 'bad feeling' about the librarian who worked there, who promised nothing but repetitive work and zero career progression. She turned down the job offer but wondered if she would regret it.

SOLUTION
Mary approached other colleges and offered herself on a casual basis as a term-time only staff member; having worked like this for a year, she identified a college that suited her. She applied for permanent work there and as a result of the variety of her experience was offered work.

Case study: 'Diving in too fast'

Some people, enticed by the dream of how they can change their lives, set off at such a pace that it is like a marathon runner starting off at a 100 metre runner's speed. They succumb to cramp, fall off the track or simply run wildly off course.

Sue had an elderly mother to care for, three children and a full-time job, but wanted to take the career advancement being offered within her present company, which involved greater demands but greater financial rewards. After six months she was flagging due to tiredness and trying to do too much.

Solution

She had to reassess the situation, delegate some tasks to her children, enlist support from other family members and use some of her extra pay to get help in the house.

'Going with the flow'

Some people might not describe this as a pitfall; it may seem rather a positive, even life-enhancing way to go. Well, it might be and it might work, but I have the feeling it probably works only if you are really observant, disciplined and focused. What I mean is this – to go with the flow, you need to know a bit about the flow and be ready and able to follow it, geared up with a great sense of self-awareness and what you need to make life meaningful for you. So if you are all these things, it might work. But beware, going with the flow is often an excuse for waiting for things to happen or doing nothing, and in my experience that rarely works.

A last motivational digression

I'm a less than skilled driver, and I say that without any embarrassment, because I know what I am good at and don't mind being bad at a couple of things. I can even maintain honestly that I choose not to be an excellent driver, because the process of becoming an advanced driver does not really interest me. The process required to be a good enough driver worked for me because it got me where I wanted to go (passing my test) and gets me where I want to go now.

Perhaps though, this is one of the keys to motivation – wanting to do what it takes (the process) to get beyond just getting there. Let's try an example – many people want a great job, paying great money, with great appreciation; that's only one side of the equation though, one part of the wanting – that's the goal. The other part is 'doing anything that it takes to achieve that goal' with all the effort, determination and discomfort this includes. The sum looks like this:

The process – finding out what you want/checking it is available/working out steps to achieve it/taking the steps/being persistent/sustained wanting – equals progress and eventually the goal.

So here's the equation:

PROCESS + PROGRESS = GOAL

If it is hard to find exactly what you want to do, it is just as hard to make it happen; many fall at the first hurdle or give up on the first side of the equation. It is not lack of backbone, it is sometimes life wearing them down or pitfalls they fail to avoid or lack of flexibility to change course. You need to cultivate a sustained wanting/motivation by rewarding yourself, appreciating yourself, encouraging support from those around you, who may be doing similar things and need your support too! But most of all your wanting has to be more than a passing whim; you have to really want it enough, not just the outcome but the process, because that is part of the whole.

William Bridges, a guru on the future of work refers to lack of motivational intensity as 'driving with the brake on'. I believe that we sometimes put the brake on intentionally out of fear of the speed of change or just to trip ourselves up. But remember how you were taught to do a hill start for your driving test; you had to ease off the handbrake slowly while letting the clutch bite. Your change of career is just like a hill start, you need to focus and take it slowly once you feel the bite; fairly soon you'll be zooming.

4 The truth is really out there

The 'what else/what is there' question is possibly the main obstacle that many potential career changers face. It is a challenge that many people choose to ignore for a variety of reasons, which probably deep down hint at more painful 'what if' questions. Simply stated these go something like this:

'What if I knew or found out what was out there and it was within my grasp and I failed to grab it?'

'What if I knew or found out what was out there and there was nothing for me and I had to accept that I had to stay doing what I am doing and be miserable for ever?'

The answers to these 'what if' questions need to be dealt with frankly and brutally, as these mental states are the justification for a creeping paralysis that many people fall victim to. First, finding out what is out there for you is actually the easy part; deciding to grab hold of something is the harder part. Fear of failure or of taking a risk are at the root of this, but with a measured approach and a strong sense of purpose it becomes the best sort of calculated risk, more an exciting venture. Moreover, it doesn't have to be as risky as a tightrope walk, as there are ways of planning for safety or back-up precautions as you go along, rather like having a safety harness and a reassuring safety net.

'What if' – scenario 1

CASE STUDY
James had a good, safe job as an experienced policeman and was now working on the recruitment side. For further promotion he needed more training in human resources or to go back on to the operational side; that would involve shift work again, which he no longer wanted. He wanted a new career direction outside the police force, which could build on his skills and experience. He had police training on defusing violent situations and in

running customised training courses for police staff, but he had no formal qualifications in training outside the force. He had the option to reduce his hours to four days a week prior to early retirement at 45 years; as he was 42, this gave him three years to set in motion a new career plan.

After some discussion of his options, I suggested the idea of a 'portfolio' career for the future. A portfolio career is when someone chooses to combine a number of small jobs to make up one career; they can be linked or completely different and are ideal for people who like variety and have varied skills and experience. (More about this in Chapter 6). Within his portfolio James could do some training consultancy work on a contractual/self-employed basis and some part-time college teaching to students on public services courses (courses for young people aiming for careers in the police, fire service, ambulance service, armed forces etc). As he would have a police pension he knew he would have a base salary while he set up his new career.

James could see that this type of career change was within his grasp, but he needed to retain his earning capacity in his main police job while gaining qualifications and experience to launch his new career direction at 45. This was the strategy we devised.

THREE-YEAR CAREER CHANGE STRATEGY FOR JAMES

FIRST YEAR
James decided to start by doing a formal training qualification through evening study at a local college. The IPD (Institute of Personnel and Development – the main professional body for human resources and training) Certificate in Training Practice was perfect as it involved three hours per week over a year and helped him back up and validate his real life training experience.

SECOND YEAR
He decided that it would be useful to pick up a basic further education (FE) teaching qualification and so he started a City & Guilds FE teaching qualification, again at college, through evening study.

THIRD YEAR
He started to create training packages in areas of his expertise with materials and formats that he knew he could offer. He contacted different firms of training consultants and started to market himself to them. He made himself available one day a week to start working as a self-employed training consultant, as his police hours were flexible. He also contacted local colleges running public services courses and offered to be available on a free consultancy basis to gain valuable experience. As a result of this he was offered six hours a week paid teaching, which he did alongside his four day a week police career.

THE OUTCOME

On taking early retirement at 45 James had successfully launched a new career in two separate areas and was working two days a week as an employed college teacher and three days per week as a training consultant.

So reaching out for a new career opportunity does not have to involve great risk as long as a measured approach is taken. This is what researching what's out there is about: exploring options properly; working out a strategy; and breaking it up into manageable steps according to your own timescale. Failing to grab a career opportunity is generally due to lack of research, too vague a plan and poor self-belief. Tell yourself you are worth it and anything will be possible – it will still be a venture, but call it an adventure!

'What if' – scenario 2

There is, of course, a remote, almost infinitesimal chance that you could go to the bother of checking out what is out there for you and find that nothing is available. This generally means one of two things; firstly it might confirm for you that what you are doing is what you really want to do. This can be good, as you can start to make the most of opportunities available in that job and look for better career satisfaction there; or you can develop some other area of your life, for example hobbies or voluntary work.

Secondly, it often means that you have placed insurmountable restrictions on any career change possibility; people invariably do this to reassure themselves of their own burdensome life. For some people so-called insurmountable restrictions can be overcome; others, for their own reasons, really don't want to find a solution. The following two examples will show you what I mean.

Insurmountable restrictions that were overcome

CASE STUDY

Sarah wanted to gain some qualifications, as she eventually wanted to train for sick children's nursing. She was starting at zero as she had very poor schooling due to ill health. She was a single parent on Income Support and had three young children, all below school age. She had no close family nearby. She needed to start by building up some confidence to help her believe she could study; a basic skills Maths and English course at a local college would help with this and would be free of charge, but childcare would be a problem. Her nearest college had no crèche facility, but by talking to other young mothers at a toddler group she was able to negotiate a childcare trade, whereby she 'minded' another mother's two children one afternoon a week, in return for a free afternoon for herself. She used this time to enrol on a basic skills course.

Having done that for a year she was ready to enrol on some GCSE courses but again this would involve more hours of college study and more problems over childcare arrangements. She found that a flexible study scheme for GCSEs at her local college would work for her as she could study at home via study packs sent to her. She studied in the evenings when her children were asleep. She found it hard but was supported by telephone tutorials with her tutors, which kept her on track. Two years later she had the entry level qualifications for diploma level nursing training. For more about flexible/distance learning see Chapter 5.

Insurmountable restrictions that might have been overcome

CASE STUDY

Emma worked part-time as a secretary and had two school-age children. She had decided she wanted to train for occupational therapy but needed to gain A-level qualifications and preferably some caring experience. Her husband worked shifts so evening study would be difficult. She could not afford to give up her job.

Caring experience through hospital volunteering would be easy to acquire, but she found it difficult to find the time for this. She could have taken one day a week to study one A-level at a time over two years, but household chores seemed overwhelming on her days off. She decided to leave this career plan for a time in the future.

Emma did have real restrictions, but it was more than likely that it was the timing or her desire for a change that was wrong. Invariably, though, putting it off for insubstantial reasons means putting it off for good, or means poor motivation. Often this gives people an excuse for staying where they are and not going for their dreams, as they can say:

'Well, I'm just stuck because of my circumstances.'

'I'm so unlucky. It's not my fault that I can't do what I want.'

Possible ways round Emma's situation might have been: as a volunteer, she could have decided the time commitment she could offer, and it could be flexible and fitted around various circumstances; better delegation and redistribution of household chores amongst the whole family might have freed up some time for her A-level study.

The 'what ifs' will kill you if you let them!

The point worth realising is, that these 'what ifs' will kill you (metaphorically speaking!) if you let them and they are more often a sign of weak motivation. So if you find yourself mentally inundated with 'what if' scenarios take a moment to contemplate what you really want, how much you want it, and picture yourself having what you want. With a strong sense of purpose the 'what ifs' will be squeezed out like water from a holey sponge and you will be ready to build your own career planning strategy. More about motivation in Chapter 10. Finally on what ifs, the timing of any career plan/strategy is vital, as mentioned in the previous chapter, so this has to be carefully considered. Taking on too much, too fast, can result in a sense of failure and unwillingness to try again, so beware of this.

The unexplored planet

Be an alien for a moment and think what you would do if you landed here on earth. You would probably peep out first, start looking round close to the spaceship and then start going further afield. If the natives looked friendly you would talk to them and find out more; you might try out earth experiences like football or libraries or sleeping! It's unlikely that having travelled all the way here you would just stay in the spaceship looking out of the windows, waiting for something to happen.

Many people say they want to explore other career paths but do it by staying in the spaceship, waiting for something to happen and, if something does happen, they take the first thing that is offered. The key to finding out what is out there is to step out of the spaceship. The next thing to do is to start looking round nearby and, once that has been explored, going a little further; talking to people and trying out experiences can be done next. And so, a good plan for exploring your real career options looks something like this:

start looking + looking some more + talking to people + experiences =

KNOWING WHAT'S OUT THERE

Let's break this down into a simple plan.

Start looking

It's much easier to check out real career change possibilities that are available locally first. This makes sense as for some people local availability is crucial, and generally it is less overwhelming to start this way. Do something obvious first – buy some newspapers! It is worth buying a good local paper that has job adverts to start with; make it a research project to find out who the main local employers are, what kind of staff they are recruiting, who pays the best, what type of training they are offering. It is a good idea to do this over a six-month period so that you begin to get a feel for what is happening locally. Don't just read the adverts but send for the job details, even if you're not ready to apply for anything yet. Start comparing different employers and how they recruit, what they want and what they are offering. Start building up a file of job titles and employers that interest you; don't worry if you are mismatched by way of qualifications or experience, just open yourself up to more possibilities.

Look some more

Next try and buy a regional paper that has good job adverts and do the same over a period of months. You are now broadening your knowledge of jobs and their requirements. Buy a selection of national papers and see what kind of jobs are advertised in different papers. It is easy to do this quite quickly if you have access to the Internet as most good newspapers have websites with recruitment pages. Make a note of any recruitment agencies that seem to be advertising regularly in job or geographical areas that interest you. It may be time to look at international or global opportunities, which might be advertised in major national newspapers, on the Internet or through some of the recruitment agencies.

Talk to people

You may have some contact names from your job adverts or you may know someone who knows someone who does a job similar to those you might be interested in. Make a shortlist of jobs that have caught your attention from your 'just looking' research and then brainstorm a list of people who you could talk to about these jobs. Try friends and acquaintances first and get new contacts from them. Create a questionnaire with everything you want to ask about your selected jobs and use this to interview your contacts. Your questions should include:

- What is this job really like?
- What makes someone good at this job?
- What skills/experience are needed?
- What training is normally required?

- Is the training part of the job or done prior to the job as part of a required qualification?
- Are there any shortcuts to this kind of work?
- What are the pay and prospects?
- What is the availability of this kind of work?

After doing this you should begin to have an idea of what would suit you and you may have good contacts for future work.

Experiences or 'trying it on'

If you have ever ordered from a mail order catalogue you will know how chancy it is to buy something on the basis of a picture and a few lines of text. Having talked to someone in the job, the next thing to do is to ask if you can 'try it on'. This might seem a difficult request, but 'work shadowing' or 'work trials' are possible with good employers. In some occupations it is virtually compulsory that you have sampled the job in some way; for example for therapy careers in hospitals it is recommended that you visit a therapy department or that voluntary work is undertaken. Here are two ways you might broach the subject:

'I'm really interested in a career in environmental health and am considering applying to university for related courses. I'm sure you would agree that it is vital to gain on-the-ground experience and I wonder if it would be possible to work shadow an environmental health inspector for a day or two. I'd be happy to do any routine work to help or act just as an observer.'

'I'm keen to do this kind of work and would be happy to offer you a free work trial of one week to show you what I can do and to see if we suit each other.'

As previously mentioned there is a great range of voluntary work available in almost every conceivable job area, through which skills and experience can be gained and suitability for different kinds of work can be verified. For more on this see Chapter 6.

By exploring jobs and careers in this realistic way you are far more likely to uncover something that is right for you, and by developing your 'networking' skills, that is, talking to people and making use of contacts, you will have increased your chances of good career opportunities coming your way, by opening yourself up to other possibilities.

However, if you set off on this exploring without doing some elementary assessment of what you want or need from a new career you will just get hopelessly lost. Let's say that as an alien you arrive in your space-ship, have a bumpy landing and succumb to amnesia. Going off exploring without some sense of your self, without an idea of what your strengths are, and without a list of your criteria for job satisfaction is like being an alien with amnesia!

Too often people can get bogged down in the detail of what they want from a job, when the 'big picture' of what they want is far more important and revealing. Here's an example. Lucy had some detailed specifications for what she wanted from a career. She said she needed high earning power but she could only study part-time as she worked in the evenings. When we discussed what was most important to her in a job, she decided it was to be autonomous and work flexibly on her own for the most part and to communicate/make things clear. She wanted to aim high as she was naturally competitive. While the detail was important, so was the 'big picture', and this led to her looking at careers in law, in particular work as a barrister. Sometimes, 'big picture' thinking can broaden out ideas and lead to better possibilities.

To gain a sense of what the 'big picture' might be for you, try asking yourself the question, 'What is important to me about my career?' Write as many answers as possible to this question (at least ten). Divide the list into two parts: 'detail' and 'big picture'. Have a look at the detail statements and dilute them down to even more detail. Look at them again and examine them for any 'big picture' intimations as well; add any more you find to the 'big picture' list. This is how one person's lists might look.

Alien 1

Details	Big picture
I want a well-paid job	I have a large family to support
I want a high-status job	I want people to look up to me
I want variety	I am easily bored
I want to be an expert	I want people to look up to me
I don't want to work too hard	I like an easy life
I want to travel	I am easily bored
I don't want stress	I like an easy life

Exploring options with these criteria in mind will be a much more thorough process. Matching yourself 'warts and all' against any potential career is much more effective if you have undertaken an honest evaluation of what you want. Let's take a possible job for Alien 1, say event/conference management, and see how it matches. This would fulfil many of Alien 1's criteria, allowing opportunities for travel, variety and a certain expertise; however, there would undoubtedly be stress involved in dealing with people, but reasonable financial reward. Alien 1 might match himself against this career and give it a score of eight out of ten. Another career, like accountancy, might score less well in some areas but better in others, and Alien 1 might score it at seven out of ten.

In simple terms this is what realistic career matching is about, but it is only the first step in your exploration of potential careers. You should find out about training and qualifications required for different jobs, and unless you are prepared to do what it takes to get into the career of your choice, being a good match will not be enough.

Take the example of Alien 2, who decided she matched a career as an actuary perfectly: she was good at Maths and interested in working in the insurance industry; she could work on her own and was good with computers. Her 'big picture' thinking was that she wanted a serious profession for self-respect and a high-status job for financial independence. It looked a good match, but on finding out that she would need to do three years of degree-level study for a Maths or Actuarial Science degree, and that she would need preferably a first-class Honours or 2:1 classification, she decided it might be higher than her best mathematical attainment level. She looked at similar financial careers as an alternative and decided to keep her options open.

It is important to keep your 'You' map from Chapter 2 as well as your detail and 'big picture' criteria when you go exploring, and don't worry if you take a few wrong turnings along the way – it's all part of the experience. In fact, there's a lot to be said for occasionally 'going with the flow'; I'm not recommending drifting aimlessly, but often when exploring unexpected jewels can be found. Perhaps you are talking to a social worker who suggests you talk to a probation worker who suggests you talk to a youth justice worker. Social workers work with all kinds of people to make sure they get the level of care they need. Probation workers work with people in prison or recently released from prison, helping to ensure they do not reoffend. Youth justice workers help and support young people between the ages of 11 and 16 years, who may have initial criminal offences, to prevent them reoffending. It could be that following this flow you come upon a more suitable career than you had expected.

Give me money

Some people feel embarrassed to make this one of their criteria for a career change, others are very honest about it. Whichever, it is generally a factor in deciding on a change of career, so accurate information on the earning potential of various jobs is essential. It is unfortunately true that jobs are rarely paid on their value to society, so that in general caring jobs are paid less than commercial jobs. Jobs that have a scarcity value in terms of skills or experience also generally pay better than jobs that have a more universal skill level. For example, there are currently shortages nationally of maths and science teachers so financial training incentives are being offered; there is still a skills shortage in computer careers so highly-skilled computer expertise is rewarded highly.

It is still the case that people who do a more 'hands-on' job, whether in engineering, caring or horticulture, are paid less than those with a management responsibility. It is also fairly well proven that, although a university degree does not guarantee a great or well-paid job, a university degree holder has greater earning potential than someone without one. Therefore, if anyone asks me how to ensure better career prospects for themselves, I have to help them to consider some kind of university course as potentially a good idea.

Apart from this, money is paid for uniqueness, by way of skills, experience or qualifications, so it is vital that you can identify any unique skill or ability you have. An example of this would be my mother who, although wonderful and qualified in many ways, has a unique skill, which she has never had the chance to use. As she was brought up in India she had the choice of learning French or Urdu at school and chose Urdu; she came to England in her twenties and has never used this fairly uncommon skill. If she had lived in an area with a large Asian community she might have used this skill in a number of career areas – social services, the courts, citizens' advice, community work, teaching etc. Language skills are of course useful in many ways but people are put off by the length of time needed to gain fluency. However, sign language can be learned in a year or two, through evening or daytime study, and can lead to many interesting career areas. A recent job advert for travel representatives abroad asked for language skills and included signing in the list of useful languages.

But back to the money question. Once you have explored and found out some suitable careers, the price paid for them is a valid deciding factor. You might gain information on pay from your talks with job contacts, but otherwise a good source of information of current pay scales for most careers can be found in *Occupations* by COIC. Finding a career that fulfils your job satisfaction criteria but does not allow you to support yourself or other people you care for financially can be extremely frustrating, so make sure you check this out. It may be that you structure your career change plan differently and decide to aim higher, or that you use voluntary work as a way of gaining life satisfaction. Let's look at two examples.

Alien 3 had explored successfully and had decided that a career as a support worker with adults with learning disabilities was an ideal career change for him – he wanted to feel he did something that mattered and made a difference. He discovered that pay scales often started at £4 per hour, which would not allow him to deal with his own financial obligations. Better pay might be possible if he did excessive amounts of weekend work, but this did not seem the best answer to him. He decided that a different route into working in the area might be through recognised social work training such as the Diploma in Social Work. This, however, would involve two years of full-time study and he would have to show care work experience to be accepted on this course, as well as A-level or an equivalent qualification.

He decided to put off a quick career change for a more planned approach; he continued in his present employment and took two years to gain the required qualification level. He chose to study an A-level in Psychology and an Open College B unit in Care (equivalent to A-level standard). At the same time he worked as a volunteer once a month on a Sunday in a variety of social care placements locally, developing invaluable skills and experience with adults with a range of disabilities. In addition, he took voluntary advocacy training, which prepared him to act as an advocate for adults with mental health problems. Alongside this, he opened an individual learning account (ILA – see Chapter 8) through his local TEC and began to save regularly for his career change so that he could afford to do the Diploma in Social Work; the TEC gave him £150 for the first £25 he saved. (More about this in Chapter 8.)

Two years later he started his Diploma in Social Work course and two years further on he started work as a social worker on the social worker salary grade, which is higher than the support worker grade. A four-year time-scale for this career change example might seem irritating, but getting where you really want to go on your terms means that sometimes a quick-fix solution is not the best answer.

A fairly similar situation, with a different solution, is the one Alien 4 found herself in – she wanted a more caring career but had a mainly administration background and a job that paid quite well. She could not afford the substantial salary drop a care support worker job would entail and did not wish to take on prolonged study to train as a social worker. On exploring career options locally, she noticed that charity administration work as a fundraising manager or as an administration support worker was quite often advertised and only slightly less well paid than her current work. She needed to work as a volunteer with local charities to gain 'on-the-ground experience' and she took an accountancy technician (AAT – Association of Accounting Technicians) qualification at evening college to fine tune her financial skills. A year later she gained a post with a local charity, for which she had already done voluntary fundraising, as a fundraising organiser. She did not mind that she had a less 'hands-on' care role, because she felt she could 'make a difference' through using her administrative skills in a more satisfying way.

Taking a step back before going forward

Invariably, changing career will have some financial implications and it is likely that even the most perfect career change will involve a slight dip in financial pay off; this is why some forward planning can help and a personal career development savings plan such as an ILA can be useful. It is quite common for someone restarting in a new career area to have to begin in a trainee role with, understandably, a slight drop in income. It is always worth remembering that, although pay is important in a job, it is only a detail in the big picture and is only one of the 'pay offs' you will get from doing what you really want to do.

The low pay trap

Without placing too much importance on the pay question, it is clear that for many people the reason for seeking a better job is to improve their earning potential. In simple terms there are probably six proven ways to improve an individual's earning power:
1. Opening yourself up – exploratory surgery
2. Unique personality/temperament attributes
3. Better, more specific and higher qualifications
4. Real 'employer-valued' experience
5. Unique skills
6. Knowing someone.

Opening yourself up – exploratory surgery

Briefly, because this has been covered already, this means that you first need to know yourself and what you really have to offer – your unique package of skills, qualities and experience. It will involve peeling off the brown paper wrapping and string you have hidden yourself beneath and deciding to make yourself a more appealing package – this is called selling yourself. You need to think more positively and eliminate negative thoughts and you will also have to explore what is out there for you.

Unique personality/temperament attributes

You will have uncovered these by doing your 'You' map audit. You will have realised that any future career probably needs to fit round your key personal qualities and individuality. By doing this you will find that you are better at what you do and work more effectively, and this normally means an increase in earning potential.

Better, more specific and higher qualifications

Let's start with what 'better' might mean. It's probable that a maths and english qualification and two or three other subjects at GCSE or equivalent is a good minimum level to aim for so, if you are below this level, have a look at ways of reaching it. This could mean evening classes, weekend college or flexible learning through home study or it could mean NVQ training to at least Level 2 (and preferably Level 3) through workplace training or other work-based qualifications that are equivalent to GCSEs.

'Better' qualifications help you keep up with the pace of change in the world of work and keep you employable; they also mean that you can move from job to job easily, because you have a proven level of education, a kind of educational passport. They don't of course make you a 'better' person, because your individual package and your experience still count for more. Research with employers proves time and time again that personal qualities such as being willing to learn, being reliable and self-confident are the most desirable attributes, but the amazing bonus of gaining qualifications is that:

1. You get shortlisted for job interviews, because employers often use qualification levels as a short cut for shortlisting applicants, especially when they have a lot of applications.
2. You attract notice from your present employer, who might offer you 'better' career prospects on hearing you have been self-motivated enough to improve your qualifications.

3. You end up feeling 'better' about yourself by returning to study and/or achieving qualifications and almost unconsciously send out 'better' vibes.

Knowing you can do a job that is advertised and knowing you can show this at an interview is unfortunately not enough to put yourself in the frame for that job. You need to be selected for an interview by what is still a fairly arbitrary process, which normally involves someone scanning through application forms or CVs looking for defined criteria such as the minimum qualification levels set for the job. Not being in possession of the requisite qualifications can result in you being sifted out, even before you reach the interview stage.

Deciding to return to study and gain qualifications often acts as a jump start for people; it improves their self-confidence, their demeanour, their focus and makes an employer 'think again' about someone they might have pigeonholed. Here's an example: Luke had been working for some time with a manufacturing company and had made good career progress, but it had suddenly come to a halt. He had become negative about his career prospects and believed he had been passed over for better jobs, which he knew he could have managed. He wanted to be considered for junior management positions but his company was not sure of his ability to make this step.

He enrolled on an Introductory National Examining Board for Supervisory Management qualifications Certificate course (NEBs) at a local college on one evening a week and learnt about the key areas of managing people, finance and resources; he found it fascinating and went on to take further NEBS qualifications. He started to make suggestions in his workplace and when they worked his managers began to look at him differently. His own attitude had changed so much that customers sought his advice and eventually a customer offered him a management position, as did his current employer.

Seizing the opportunity to gain better qualifications actually puts you in charge and gives you a self-confidence charge. Changing the status quo of your present employment by enrolling for a course gives you the chance to reassess and stretch yourself and makes people around you also reassess you.

Real 'employer-valued' experience

Again research shows that there are certain experience packages that employers value and if you spend time reading job adverts you quickly get the picture of what they value. What follows is rather a random list of what they seem to want by way of experience.

Employer-valued experience list

Previous experience in that specific career area, eg catering experience for a chef or nail extensions experience for a beauty therapist.
Information technology (IT) or computing experience, eg specific knowledge of how to use spreadsheets, databases, AppleMac computers or desktop publishing, as relevant to the job description.
Change management experience; this is often referred to in job adverts, and simply means that applicants would be expected to have experience in dealing with a changing employment environment with a proven adaptability to new demands, systems or company objectives.
Experience of working under pressure and ability to perform to deadlines and imposed targets; this is also sometimes referred to as 'achievement orientated' in adverts, meaning that experience of working in a competitive, pressurised atmosphere is highly valued.
Customer service/sales experience and direct contact with the public, including dealing with difficult or problem people, is a prized skill.
Motivational skills and experience are in demand in either a training context or in social care situations with young people, for example for teachers and youth workers supporting and encouraging demotivated pupils.
Problem solving experience in any career/job area is valued by employers, who often say 'Don't come to me with problems! Bring me solutions'.
Ability to work unsupervised or 'on own initiative' is a frequently expressed job advert requirement.
Telephone experience, especially in the expanding call centre area, is valued.
Language skills, including all global languages, or those of ethnic UK groups and sign language are additional extras in many job specifications.

The two obvious points to note from this list are that:

1. Experience has to be proven by what you have done and how you can show it.
2. The ability to work well with people, either in a service context or through teamwork with colleagues, is crucial and so people experience is king.

Experience in these areas is the detail in the employability equation. The big picture for many employers is to make money, and if you can prove you will help with this in real terms then ultimately you are very employable.

Unique skills

These are simply any skills or experience you have, which are transferable from what you have done before, that could be considered an asset in other types of employment. Examples of this might be fluency in a language, being tall for basketball, being unafraid to stand up in front of large audiences or being able to understand quantum physics.

Knowing someone

There is an element of luck in career choices and, sometimes, knowing someone can make the difference. It can help with information on a particular job or by giving you a contact for an unusual career. It is sometimes considered unfair to get a job as a result of a personal contact, but it still happens, and it's better to accept this and use it to your advantage. Networking is the term for this skill (see also page 79) and it can be used, at least, to get you through the door of a career opportunity – after that, you'll be on your own!

What you can tell from what you do now

Obviously what you are doing currently or have done previously can provide clues to proven experience or transferable skills, or what you do or don't want to do in the future, so it is worth looking rather carefully at this and analysing it. I took up a position in a university library after a career break. It was perfect for me at that time because it was termtime only and 16 hours per week over four days, finishing at lunchtime, when I would chase home to meet my school-age children. It gave me the bonus of provable experience, transferable skills and definite signals for my new career direction: I could prove I could deal with people (including difficult customers); I developed IT skills using databases and I could work well in a team. I realised that I liked the help and advice bit of the job best, and working in an education context, and this pointed me in the direction of careers advisory work.

Take some time to analyse what you are doing now or have done previously and you will find similarly valuable information for your career change planning.

Help yourself to help

When you are setting out on this career change adventure it helps to know the kind of things that have helped other people, so here is a short list of key sources of 'first steps' help and advice.

Short qualification courses

Many people fear a return to study because they have minimal or no qualifications. A good first start for someone with little English and/or Maths confidence is a foundation course. These are offered at most colleges and are designed for adults who lack confidence in these areas. They can be studied in the evenings, daytime or often at a weekend and normally involve three hours a week in a class with some home study. They normally have small class sizes and individual support by tutors. These classes can change people's lives by letting them believe they can actually cope with study!

Colleges also offer specific 'Return to study' courses as confidence building tasters to tempt adults back into education – these may be called Access or foundation courses.

Many colleges are piloting weekend courses, which are often short courses in computing or basic skills such as English/Maths or basic counselling, to tempt people to develop their own skills and interests, which in turn might lead to new career opportunities.

Short interest/confidence building courses

Sometimes a hobby or interest can provide a springboard for a new career or a way in to a new qualification. For example, someone might take a short course in reflexology for personal enjoyment and then go on to qualify as a reflexologist through a reflexology diploma.

Equally self-development courses available at many colleges, such as assertiveness and positive thinking, can build confidence to move on to other areas or simply help you to be more effective in your present job.

Good careers advice

Most colleges have advisers who can help you in deciding the right level of course to start with and course tutors will be able to discuss the delights and demands of different courses.

Independent careers advice for adults is available locally through companies contracted by the government. An interview with a professional careers adviser, who will know all the local/regional employment and college situations, can open you up to all your own potential and can help you plan the best way forward. This service is normally free to unemployed people or at a small cost to those who are working.

Career/life coaching

Some people need an ongoing support system from someone who can encourage and motivate them to make the changes that will make them happy. Coaching is normally through a telephone contact once a week, over a short or long period, and has been enormously successful for people who need to invest in their own career but never make the time. Coaching gives them an independent person 'in their corner', fighting to help them to be in peak condition in their present career or in making a career change. Having someone like a coach in your life can help you to put into action the things you want by getting the best advice, bouncing ideas around and paying attention to your own needs. By investing your time and money with a coach you are investing in your own success. Costs vary, but on average it will cost about £140 for three half-hourly phone sessions with a coach. More about this in Chapter 10.

Occupational psychologists/careers consultants and psychometric testing

Occupational psychologists can also help you determine the best career direction and use special types of assessment tests to find out your key abilities and personality type; this can help focus a career change on your real strengths. Tests can often surprise people by uncovering unrealised gifts or simply confirming perceived talents. Test results can be used to promote those in employment or as an indication of ability for higher education courses. A good example of this was Henry, who had no school qualifications as he had moved around a lot when he was young. In later life he passed an IQ test with an extremely high score and was pronounced 'off the range' in a numerical psychometric test by a professional occupational psychologist. As a result of this evidence he was offered a place on a degree course in accountancy without any other qualifications.

Libraries/local college/university prospectuses/ the Internet

These are all sources of good, free information, so make sure you use them. There is more about the Internet in Chapter 10.

And finally, a quick mention of the pain barrier that you will have to go through before you can really start to make things happen for you.

Easing the pain

The word pain stands here for all the things you may think are in your way. Typically these might be the cost of studying in your personal time, financial or problems of care, ill health or disabilities. The limitations of what is available for you locally can also be part of this pain. This type of pain is probably like a growing pain – essential. Pain relief is as follows.

The time it will take

We use up a lot of our time doing nothing or moaning about how we would like things to be. Calculate the weekly time spent on this and resolve to use it in a meaningful way.

The money it will cost

Further study might be free depending on your circumstances or it might cost you anything from £100 for an average GCSE course to £1000 for a professional level course. Most evening and weekend college courses are around the £100 mark and can be paid in instalments if necessary. Day-time Access courses are normally free for adults. Foundation-level basic skills or university Access/foundation courses are generally free. Be ready to shop around a bit, as costs can vary from college to college; but remember, spending money on yourself for a tangible result that is life enhancing is a good habit to get into.

Childcare/carer problems

Some colleges have a free crèche facility, while others can help with childcare costs from their own Access funds (money given to colleges by the government to help adult students). It is also worth exploring all the alternatives – babysitting clubs, after-school clubs, sharing with friends and begging family members. Home study would still be an option if you simply cannot get out, see 'Flexible study' in Chapter 5.

Ill health and disabilities

Restrictions due to ill health or disabilities can be worked around, with additional support available from the learning support department of colleges and from disability employment advisers at local job centres. Concentrate on what you can do and plan around this, while using all the help available.

Geography

This ought not to be a problem, but we are not all entirely free to move anywhere to gain work – working around children's schools and partner's employment is a reality for many, so a positive approach is required, with thorough research of local opportunities. Be wary, nonetheless, of drawing too tight a boundary on your geographical limitations – lift sharing, bus and rail travel passes may make travelling more possible than you initially think.

So let's get back in the spaceship. You're sitting there with all the truth you've been able to find outside it. You know the types of opportunities that can work for you but you need to make some decisions to make things happen. You're going to need a plan, broken down into manageable steps, so that you can believe it is possible. That's what comes next!

CHAPTER 5

Making sense of it all or how to make the change

There was once an alien who, back in his spaceship after a rather long exploratory trip, found himself overwhelmed by all the maps and information he had collected about things he could do. However much he thought about it, he just could not decide what to do or even what to do first. He was found many years later, a rather old alien who had never again left his spaceship.

Don't be like the alien and never make the next leap into the unknown to decide what is right for you. There are all sorts of good reasons for this paralysis, but most often they boil down to:
1. You have not really taken in all your options.
2. You are scared of making the wrong decision.
3. You are not ready yet.
Let's begin with number one.

Finding out what is out there is not the same as knowing what is best

If you have seriously been collecting information about ways to change career you've probably amassed a suitcase full of leaflets from colleges and training centres about all types of courses or training. Making sense of all these, and ultimately how they will help you get where you want to go, can be baffling and mind numbing. What you need first is a kind of encyclopaedia of these types of options with easy to grasp details, so that's what I will try to give you next. This list may not be 100 per cent comprehensive because, as I write, new courses are being developed. But it is as full a list as possible.

Access courses

These are courses run by most colleges of further education and are designed for adults who wish to improve their qualifications, return to study, build their confidence up or simply find out what they are capable of. They are generally run during the day, probably taking no more than 15 hours per week as people in receipt of Income Support and Job Seekers Allowance are only allowed to study under 16 hours a week. They can be eight, 16 or 32 weeks in duration; 32 weeks is a full college year. Access courses are free as they are subsidised by the government, which wants us all to return to learning and update our qualifications (see 'Lifelong learning', page 12). For many Access courses no prior qualifications at all are needed.

I have to restrain myself when I talk about Access courses as I am inclined to talk about them as if they can change the world. They have certainly contributed to changes in the lives and careers of people throughout this country simply because they work so well. I know this from personal experience with people I have helped, who say that they can hardly believe the transformation that they can trigger. I use the word 'trigger' because, clearly, the Access course does not itself make someone great, it just helps someone realise that they can be great in some ways!

Access courses work for several reasons:

1. Students on these courses are all in the same boat; they are adults who wish to make a change of some kind to their lives and they support and encourage one another.

2. Tutors for these courses like teaching adults as they are generally a well-motivated bunch. This means that the whole learning experience is imbued with an exhilarating yearning for learning.

3. Students study at their own pace and start at the level that is right for them.

4. The structure of Access courses normally means two to three days at college with two days clear for the other things that adults need to do. College timetables are normally fitted around school hours so most Access students start at 9–9.30am and finish at 3pm, which works for parents who are tied to school picking-up times. Some Access courses are run over a whole day and possibly one evening a week.

These courses are especially suitable for part-time workers, job sharers, people wishing to return to work after a parenting or other break, single parents on low income or Income Support, the unemployed or those who have finished work due to illness or disability. Frequently, those who work at weekends find they can fit in two or three days study, and some employers have released employees to do these types of courses as they are free. Here are three examples of typical Access course students – there are many, many more.

Case study: Young mother

This woman had one school-age child and one at nursery three days a week. She chose a vocational Access course (that is, one that prepared her for a new vocation/career) in Beauty Therapy with a view to returning to employment with new skills and experience in the future. She gained the requisite qualifications (NVQs, see page 74) in one year, but went on for a higher level NVQ for a second year and then gained work, on a part-time basis, in a health and beauty clinic.

Case study: Working man

This man worked in an alarm and security company, having started as an apprentice and worked his way upwards. He realised that technological changes meant that he needed to 'upskill' on the electronics side; he took an Access course for electronics at a higher level than he had covered on his apprenticeship; his employer agreed to release him two days a week for the 16-week course.

Case study: Man without formal qualifications

This person had worked in the building trade and was ready for a change, but believed he had no options. Starting with an Access course for basic foundation Maths and English (see page 65), he built up confidence and eliminated his fears about studying as an adult. He combined this with self-employed bricklaying while he built up the foundations for his new career direction. After a year he moved on to a Computer Installation and Repair Access course that took up one day a week for 16 weeks; at the same time he did a basic computer course so that he could use a computer himself. Following his 16-week course he started a City & Guilds Diploma in Computer Applications. At the end of two years he had basic qualifications in Maths and English and qualifications that meant he could build, repair and maintain computers and deal with basic problems that computer users might encounter. He started a new job as a computer technician after completing his course. The most interesting thing about this man was that he suffered a lot of negative advice from friends and his partner, who kept on asking him, 'What do you want to do that for?', so he had to be totally self-motivated to reach his own goal. Interestingly, he made his decision to go for the first course on 'worst-case scenario' grounds. What this means is that he might have done just the foundation course and gained qualifications in English and Maths – how could that have harmed him?

In most cases doing a course of any kind will, at worst, just be a small waste of time. Making a wrong decision is not fatal; avoiding making a decision can be lethal, if not fatal, because stagnation is close to death.

Back to Access

It might be useful for you to know the four main types of college Access courses.

Foundation-type basic skills Access courses

These are normally for people without qualifications in Maths and English, those who feel unsure about these basic skills or those who had real problems with these subjects at school. Class sizes are normally small and students can be at different levels. Volunteer tutors often help students individually, which can be very beneficial. Maths can cover basic principles of Maths and numeracy up to pre-GCSE level. English can cover basic literacy, essay and letter writing and spelling up to pre-GCSE. Teachers and tutors on these courses can advise on the readiness of students for GCSE courses. Many students go on to GCSE study from these courses.

'Return to study' Access

These are for people with low GCSE/GCE grades or no memory of what they gained at school (this is very common!); they are a new start at studying in a highly conducive adult atmosphere. Many colleges offer Open College qualifications on these courses (see page 74).

This type of Access course can be for someone who just wants to gain qualifications, try out studying again or build confidence for something else, say a higher course or a quick career change (see page 77). Most universities accept OCA as equivalent to GCSE standard, but they would want a higher level qualification such as A-levels (see page 71) or OCB (Open College B – see page 74) in addition to the OCAs.

Vocational Access courses

Sometimes a package of OCA subjects is offered as a whole course with a clear vocational or career direction. These are normally titled 'Access to…' and are what is meant by vocational Access courses. Here is a fairly comprehensive list of 'Access to…' courses offered by colleges across the country. Variations on these themes will occur, so check local colleges and be prepared to do some phoning round for the more unusual courses. Again, in general, no prior qualifications are needed for these Access courses.

Vocational Access courses

Access to Accounts	This normally covers an Association of Accountancy Technicians course at Foundation, Intermediate or Technician level; the latter can lead to higher level professional accountancy training. Students with Foundation or Intermediate level can progress into jobs as Trainee Accountancy Technicians in finance departments or accountancy firms. This is a good job for logical, numerical people who have good organisational skills.
Access to Agriculture	Normally these are short courses in agriculture and farm-related areas, which can lead to skilled farm work or farm management.
Access to Art	These courses can lead to university art courses. Some students gain confidence from doing craft-based art courses such as ceramics and go on to self-employment.
Access to Baking	Usually these courses are a short cut to skilled baking and confectionery.
Access to Beauty Therapy	These courses cover basic massage, facials, manicures, make-up techniques and, more recently, aromatherapy and reflexology. Common job opportunities seem to be self-employment or working in beauty salons/health farms etc.
Access to Business Administration/ Business Studies	These courses vary, but many tend to cover basic business/office skills with typing and wordprocessing. They are a short cut to most administrative jobs and students may take NVQs (see page 74) and/or other qualifications; for NVQs many students must have a workplace assessment, so some kind of work placement might be part of the course.

continued

Access to Care	These are popular courses for people who see themselves doing a more caring job and normally involve OCA in Care and perhaps Psychology and Sociology or Health Studies; students often go into care support jobs or study further and go on to nursing/social work and related jobs.
Access to Carpentry and Joinery	These are normally short cut courses for entry to careers in woodworking/furniture making or even coffin making!
Access to Catering	These courses can help people train to be qualified chefs and would lead to trainee chef/cook jobs; NVQs in Hospitality and Catering are taken.
Access to Community Radio Production	An unusual course (and not available everywhere) for a highly competitive area; it may lead to voluntary hospital radio type work or local radio opportunities, or even the big time for someone with talent.
Access to Computer Installation and Repair	These are becoming very popular courses and can be good for people who just want to build their own PC or do basic maintenance. They can be very good for people with strong practical skills and an interest in computers and can lead to self-employment or work in a support or sales role for computer firms; some students move on to higher level computer courses.
Access to Electrical Work	Short cut course to basic electrical skills, often through NVQ courses.
Access to Engineering	Different courses are available in specialised engineering areas such as welding, milling etc, or computer-aided design (CAD) courses.
Access to Gas Services Installation	Short cut course to gas services engineering for central heating and related areas.

continued

Access to Graphic Design	These can be OCA courses or higher level A-level or OCB courses and may lead into trainee work in design studios for extremely talented students or to degree courses in graphics-related areas.
Access to Hairdressing	Short cut course with NVQs in hairdressing.
Access to Holistic Therapies	This is a fairly new but popular course, which tends to cover aromatherapy and massage, facial/head massage, reflexology, counselling and first aid; students seem to go on to self-employment or holistic therapy centres/beauty salons.
Access to Horticulture	These are general gardening courses that cover all aspects of horticulture, including growing plants, techniques and landscaping; students can go into employment or self-employment or on to higher or more specialised courses such as landscape design or arboriculture (see 'Unusual jobs and courses' in Chapter 6).
Access to Information Technology	Many variations on this course – most cover wordprocessing, spreadsheets and databases at either beginner, intermediate or advanced level through OCR (see page 75) CLAIT (Computer Literacy and Information Technology) or City & Guilds courses. These courses can be used in a number of ways, whether to develop skills to put alongside a new job or to be the main part of a computer-related job.
Access to Interior Design	A newish type of course that teaches students about design, textiles, colour lighting and decorative paint techniques, which can lead to trainee jobs or higher level courses.
Access to Landscape Gardening	Similar to Access to Horticulture but more specialised.

continued

continued

Access to Legal Skills/Law	These courses can lead to ILEX (Institute of Legal Executives) qualifications, leading into trainee legal executive (a para-legal role as an assistant to a solicitor), or they can lead to A-level or OCB in Law, which in turn might lead on to university courses.
Access to Management	Normally these cover basic skills in managing people, resources and finance and are for aspiring or new managers.
Access to Medical Reception	These courses often cover basic reception/ secretarial skills relevant to work in a medical surgery or hospital and students normally take wordprocessing and office-related qualifications, which might include medical shorthand and/or an AMSPAR diploma (Association of Medical Secretaries and Practice Administrators).
Access to Motor Mechanics	Short cut to motor mechanics training.
Access to Music/ Music Technology	This is a fairly specialist area but courses are offered in some parts of the country and might be for aspiring rock musicians or record producers/technical sound staff.
Access to Nursery Nursing/Childcare	This is a very popular course and can involve a one-year certificate in childcare or the more demanding two-year BTec in Childhood Studies; work placements in childcare are normally part of the course.
Access to Nursing/ Paramedics/ Health Therapies/ Health Studies	These often contain a mix of OCA in Care/ Health Studies/Human Physiology and OCB in similar subjects or Psychology/Sociology; they lead to auxiliary, ambulance or health care support worker work in hospitals or on to nursing/occupational therapy (and related areas) university training.
Access to Office Skills	Quite similar to business administration courses with basic typing/wordprocessing and office skills.

continued

Access to Painting and Decorating	Short cut to painting and decorating job opportunities.
Access to Performing Arts/Media	These courses can cover performance skills such as acting, presenting or production, or the theory sides of these career areas. A highly competitive employment situation for these jobs means that prospective students must be high on self-belief and talent!
Access to Plumbing	Short cut to plumbing skills and jobs.
Access to Primary Teaching	These courses allow students to gain the minimum qualification level for teaching so must include Maths, English and Science at GCSE for those without them and two A-levels or equivalent in National Curriculum subjects (school subjects).
Access to Science	Good courses for people wanting interesting scientific careers; they can lead to laboratory or hospital technical jobs or on to higher university courses.
Access to Social Sciences/ Social Studies	OCA/OCB courses in subjects like Criminology, Sociology, Care and Law that can lead into support worker/assistant type jobs in social care or legal services or on to higher level related university courses.
Access to Sport/Sport Therapies	This is a very popular area and courses often cover sports coaching and community leadership or outward bound type awards and/or sports massage/human physiology and/or the sociology of sport. Qualifications gained can be A-levels/OCB/GCSE, OCA or other recognised awards from specific organisations such as the Football Association.
Access to Textiles	These courses can include weaving, knitting, embroidery, design skills etc, through a variety of qualifications; students can go on to jobs with textile firms or craft occupations or on to university courses.

continued

Access to Travel and Tourism	Students on these courses can take a variety of qualifications such as the ABTAC (Association of British Travel Agents Certificate) or OCA in Spanish or OCB in Tourism; many go on to work in travel companies or for tourist boards or on to higher level university courses.

University entry Access courses

These courses can be based at colleges or universities and may be called foundation or Year 0 courses (Year 0 being the year before Year 1 of a university degree course). They are intended to be a short cut to university for those without recognised qualifications, but who are well motivated and ready to study. They help prepare students for degree courses at university by showing them what the level of study would be like and giving them a taste of university courses that interest them.

They can be taken during the day over 15 hours or sometimes through evening study (probably one to two evenings a week). It is possible to gain a place on these courses with no qualifications at all, although many students have basic qualifications and good work experience. Students normally move on to Year 1 of degree courses. Many universities now charge tuition fees for these courses, so they are different, in that respect, from the free, college-based Access courses.

A-level courses (Advanced level)

These courses are a passport to university courses and can be taken in traditional subject areas such as English, Maths, History etc, as well as newer subjects such as Psychology, Media Studies, Sociology etc. They can be done in one year through daytime or evening courses, or over two years. Assessment is generally through a formal exam; most involve coursework. Some A-levels have a modular framework, which means you would take one module at a time and have modular tests to make up your final grade.

Distance learning/open learning/flexible study

This is a creature with many aliases so you need to be dedicated to sniff it out, but it can be one of the most effective and successful study methods for well-motivated people who cannot afford to give up their present job. Put simply, you study at home using study packs with tutorial support by correspondence or over the phone/email/Internet. Costs vary, from £100 to much more for some specialised courses. Easy payment schemes are often possible and for the unemployed or those in receipt of benefits colleges often waive tuition fees.

Many local colleges offer this as a flexible study option for GCSEs/OCA/OCB/A-levels or work-related qualifications. Students work at their own pace and it can be a wonderful option for those who work shifts, the housebound, for those with caring responsibilities or for ill or disabled people. Some colleges and universities offer access through the Internet to a 'virtual campus' with online courses and a variety of support services and facilities for students.

The best known of the distance learning providers is probably the Open University (see page 75) but many professional bodies offer qualifications this way.

The Open and Distance Learning Quality Council (ODL QC) has an excellent website (www.odlqc.org.uk/odlqc) that lists courses nationally that have been accredited for quality by the Council. The list covers interesting sounding courses from accounting to birdwatching, business management to advertising and public relations, international marketing to cartoons, consumer affairs to dyslexia, technical writing and proofreading. Make sure you check exactly what you will be getting by way of training and qualifications and what past students have gone on to do. See Chapter 9 for details.

ECDL (European Computer Driving Licence)

This misleading title is for a computer, not a driving, qualification and is intended as a multipurpose qualification that proves a student knows the basics of wordprocessing, spreadsheets, databases, desktop publishing, presentations, the Internet and email. It is supposed to be accepted throughout Europe and is therefore a good course to do; it is normally available through evening study.

Evening courses

There are so many types and levels of courses offered through evening study that it is difficult to know where to start, but they probably fall into the following categories:

1. Purely hobby/interest related, eg stained glass window etching, soft furnishing, calligraphy, photography, yoga, cake decorating, lip reading, woodwork etc (these may of course tempt someone to go on for higher qualifications or to teach these subjects – see FE Teaching Certificate on page 105).
2. Work-related qualifications such as ABTAC Travel Agency Certificate, IPD (Institute of Personnel and Development) Diploma, CIM (Chartered Institute of Marketing) Diploma, ILEX (Institute of Legal Executives) qualifications or AAT (Association of Accounting Technicians) qualifications.
3. Basic skills qualifications such as English and Maths foundation courses (normally free at most colleges) and computer qualifications.
4. A-level, GCSE and OCA/OCB courses in a variety of subjects.
5. University foundation courses for entry to degree courses.
6. University degree or HNC (Higher National Certificate) courses for students who need to carry on in paid work and study outside work hours (these may be college or university based).

The main point to remember about evening courses is that it is quite possible to improve your career prospects, train for another career, gain vital qualifications or just try out an area of interest without jeopardising your present job. Most courses cost around the £100 mark but would be free to the unemployed or those in receipt of certain government benefits.

GCSE (General Certificate of Secondary Education) courses

These courses can be offered through evening, daytime, weekend or distance learning and normally take one year. Subjects similar to the A-level range are offered (see page 71). Assessment is through a formal exam; most involve coursework.

HND/HNC (Higher National Diploma/Higher National Certificate) courses

These courses generally last for two years and are at university level with a strong vocational, work-related component. They can be studied at universities or, most often these days, at colleges of further education. Typical HND/HNC courses are Business Studies, Travel and Tourism, Sports Studies/Science, Hospitality and Catering, Computing etc. Some HND courses are called 'sandwich' – three-year courses where the middle year is spent on a work placement related to the course.

HND courses are normally full-time, while HNC courses are part-time, probably one day or two evenings a week. Most employers view HND and HNC courses as equal, even though HND students cover more units or modules than do HNC students. As these are university-level courses entry is by A-level/OCB standard or equivalent qualifications, although qualifications can be waived for outstanding applicants with relevant experience. It is possible for some HND/HNC students to 'top up' to degree level by studying for an extra year or two.

NVQ (National Vocational Qualifications) courses

These are often taken on day release from employment at a college or training centre for those needing qualifications in their work area. They are practical and very work specific and involve on-the-job assessments and a portfolio of work examples. There is no formal exam to pass an NVQ.

OCA (Open College A) certificates

The Open College is a national network of colleges with regional bases, offering certificated courses that can be delivered in colleges and are mainly designed for adult students. They are short courses, often 8, 10 or 16 weeks long, and can be studied through daytime, evening or distance learning. They are assessed through coursework and assignments and have no final exam, so they are particularly suitable for exam phobics.

Open College A (OCA) courses are roughly equivalent to GCSE standard, but shorter, often only 8, 10 or 16 weeks, which means that students can study up to eight OCA courses in a year, and this gives them a chance to 'taste' different subjects and prove that they can study at GCSE-level. Typical OCA subjects are those not usually studied at school such as Psychology, Sociology, Health Studies, Law or Criminology, or traditional subjects such as History, Spanish or Human Physiology (the new name for Human Biology).

OCB (Open College B) certificates

These courses are normally a year in duration and are considered equivalent to A-level standard if a pass of around 65 per cent is gained; for nursing training at diploma level entry a pass of 50 per cent is required. They are proof that a student can study at a higher level or is suitable for higher-level work opportunities. Subject areas include Psychology, Law, Care, Health Studies, Criminology and Sociology. Assessment is through a formal exam; most involve coursework.

OCR (Oxford and Cambridge and RSA)

This is just an exam board, but as it is the new name for the RSA (Royal Society of Arts) many colleges will have courses with this as part of the title, particularly in the computing, business technology and wordprocessing areas. The most common course is the OCR CLAIT. CLAIT stands for Computer Literacy and Information Technology and, while being a beginners course, it is in fact a minimum standard for 'computeracy' (horrible new word for computer literacy). See also ECDL on page 72.

Open University (OU)

This is the most highly regarded education provider of distance learning type courses, with full tutorial support through regionally based tutor groups and first-class study materials. The range of courses is vast, but many are academic, theoretical courses rather than vocational or work related; The OU does have some new vocationally related courses but these are rare. It can be costly to study this way but there are various payment schemes. Students typically take a number of years to work through courses.

Training suppliers/organisations/TECs

Training courses offered by the above are generally government funded. Adult retraining is offered free to those unemployed for over six months, but other courses might be funded for minority groups such as women returners, the disabled or particular ethnic groups. If you live in a particular geographical area certain courses may be available on a subsidised or free basis, so check local papers and with your local TEC (which will be in the phone directory).

Weekend College

This is something of a growth area for colleges that are trying to develop the market for courses at the weekend. The provision of courses is experimental to a certain extent and some colleges offer more than others. In general, though, the courses on offer are leisure, qualifications based and work related. Costs are similar to evening courses. Examples of courses include the unusual: tea bag folding (a type of paper folding!), Indian head massage, computing for the terrified, assertiveness, etc.

Now you have a little more detail about the study and training based options that might help you make a career change. It is of course possible to make a career change without studying or retraining for something new, but it is rare; for career development in the job you are in, see Chapter 10.

And finally, if you need advice regarding a course you wish to study, phone Learn Direct, a government-funded national service. They can consult their database and deal with course or training enquiries for any part of the country. See Chapter 9 for details.

Career changer's stages of enlightenment

Let's have a reminder of the stages a typical career changer might go through – this might be you!

Before	After
They might not have taken in what all their options really are.	They have done some exploring, collected information and, with details of different course and training options, they have begun to understand 'what is out there'.
They were scared of making the wrong decision.	They are still a little scared, but now they have more information they are beginning to think that they might be able to take some small first steps.
They weren't ready.	They are still not quite ready, but they're getting there.

It is useful to look at some ways of overcoming feelings of hesitation people often have before making a change. The pace and timing of the changes you make can make this easier, so let's consider quick, medium and slow change scenarios.

The quick change quickstep

For some people the need to escape from a job that makes them miserable, or the need to return to earning, or whatever the reason, demands that they make a quick change, and this often precludes retraining or a return to study for new qualifications. In this situation it is vital to keep an open mind and consider any possibilities and evaluate them carefully. This probably means that initially you might have to look at actual alternative job opportunities that are available to you in your present situation, with whatever skills, qualifications and experience, however minimal, you possess. You will need a clear sense of purpose and a positive, realistic view of who you are and what you have to offer. In the first place a personality and skills audit (see Chapters 1 and 3) can help, and then you need to start exploring job opportunities in the following ways.

Advertised vacancies

Go through advertised vacancies in local, regional and national papers and professional journals with a fine-tooth comb! It will mean assessing advertised vacancies on the basis of, first, whether you fit the essential criteria as listed, second, whether you have skills that might be transferable to that new job area and, third, whether the picture of the job as advertised interests you. The most important thing is to look at all vacancies, not just those in your current job area; if you match a job picture, it probably means you could do the job and enjoy it. Here are two examples.

CASE STUDY

Susan had worked in an administrative job in insurance for some time but was ready for a change; she was not really interested in further study or training, she just wanted something different. She was something of a perfectionist in her work and realised that she liked to work with minimum supervision. She had strong transferable skills from her current work – excellent keyboard and IT skills, and she was used to dealing with complex queries from customers over the phone. In her spare time Susan loved to read and she spent a lot of time in bookshops and libraries. She had reasonable GCSEs and two A-levels, one of which was English.

I suggested that she could look at jobs in publishing, libraries and bookselling, which she agreed matched her very well. During her research she noticed that some small publishing firms had advertised for administrative staff and she decided to make speculative applications (see page 80) to these firms. However, she also saw that library book suppliers in the region sometimes advertised for staff and this interested her too. She noticed one advert for a Book Annotator, a job she would never have thought she could do; however, on checking the job requirements she found that she was ideally suited by qualifications and transferable skills. This was the job advert:

**Book annotator
for Library Supply Book Company**

Interest in books needed to work in a bibliographic
department, assisting in the composition of book
descriptions from publishers' information.
Must enjoy work that requires attention to detail.
Must be able to work on own initiative and in a team.
Minimum A-level English standard, keyboard skills.
Please contact ... for an application form.

It is easy to see how Susan matched this job, but she would not have found the vacancy if she had stuck to the comfort zone of jobs similar to what she had done before. She had the confidence to go for something outside her immediate experience, but which she was perfectly suited to. She had to complete her application form in a way that showed how her transferable skills and personality were entirely suited to this new career area, and her enthusiasm for books came through at the interview. She was offered the job and made a quick-change move into a new, and more interesting, career.

CASE STUDY

Gordon was an ex-army sergeant who had no qualifications apart from basic English and Maths and some specific army qualifications. He was working as a lorry driver but was no longer enjoying it. In his spare time he ran an Army Cadet unit for about 70 young people and organised activities three nights per week and sometimes at weekends. He loved this unpaid work and had successfully developed the unit from a group of about 15 young people. He had leadership, organisational and motivational skills as well as energy and a commitment to inspiring young people. He wanted a quick change into something where he could use his personality and skills. He tried voluntary youth work over a three-month period for two or three hours per week and then applied successfully for an unqualified youth worker post advertised in the local newspaper, which was part-time and paid. He carried on doing some lorry driving alongside this part-time work, but was eventually offered a full-time contract in youth work. He undertook an in-service youth work qualification while working and became a fully qualified youth worker two years later. He still helps out with Army Cadets!

Personal contacts

If, as research shows, only about 25 per cent of jobs are advertised, then for you to gain access to the other 75 per cent you will need to do something more than look in the newspaper job sections. If you really want to explore what is out there for you it would be foolish to do it without using people you know. Putting out the word to family, friends, work colleagues, the postman, your fitness instructor, can uncover surprising job offers. It can be done in a gentle or forthright way depending on your style! You might say to a friend:

'I'm ready for a change in my job at the moment; if you hear of anything at your company in the sales area, I'd be grateful, if you let me know';

or to a work colleague:

'I need to be stretched a bit more than in my present role. If you hear of anything in…, please let me know';

or to a friend of a friend:

'Who could I contact at your organisation to discuss the chance of my joining the X department? I've realised lately that I'm not using my Y experience and skills to their full potential.'

The point here of course is that personal contacts are an untapped resource for many people and, in general, these contacts may be glad to help you or refer you to someone who can.

Networking

This is fairly similar to using personal contacts, but is often overlooked by prospective career changers. Try writing a list of the network of people you know currently or previously through your work and make a point of letting them know in discreet or obvious ways that you might be interested in something else. For example, if you deal with other companies as part of your job, you might impress them with your brilliance and open yourself up to a job offer. For example, Oliver was working for a large manufacturing firm as a marketing assistant and had good results and great customer service skills. He was largely unappreciated in his present company but, through contacts and networking, was offered a better job with better prospects by one of his customer companies.

It may also be that a contact in another company could be used by you for a speculative application to that firm. Cultivating a mentor in your present company can also help uncover better opportunities (more about this in Chapter 10).

Speculative applications

Writing to a company just because you want to work for them may sound obvious but can be overlooked by career changers. This needs to be done in a methodical way to be most effective. Blitzing employers in a wide radius with your CV may work, but you will waste a lot of paper and time for the chance of a result. Some employers may be flattered by your interest; many may be irritated. To increase the odds of success, it is better to follow my recommended strategy:

On-spec strategy

- Create a number of different CVs matched to the different jobs you wish to apply for; make sure that they are stunning visually. They should also be logical and easy to read and full of meaty content that shows off your personality, your skills and experience, and gives a real sense of what you can do for that employer. For more about this, consult my book, *Creating Winning CVs and Applications* published by Trotman in *The Express Skills Focus Series*.
- Write some great covering letters to accompany your CV. This kind of letter should be no more than two or three paragraphs long and should say clearly what you want and why you think it would be good for them to employ you.
- Use personal contacts and networking to uncover companies and named persons that you can target with your CV.
- Try and phone these named persons to find out if it is worth sending your CV to them or if you can have an informal chat about possible employment options.
- Try and get someone you know to recommend you to an employer and then send the CV and covering letter with a 'name drop' in the first sentence, eg 'Mr Skywalker from Death Star Inc. suggested I contact you'.
- Send CVs and covering letters to named contacts wherever possible.
- Follow-up action must be taken about two weeks after sending CVs if no contact from the company results. Ring and ask them if they received the CV and whether there might be a job that suits you.

Voluntary work

You may already be doing some voluntary work, whether you are on a school PTA, helping out with a Brownie pack or visiting the elderly. Often these activities have given you experience or show you have proven skills in areas other than your paid work. A quick change can be effected by using this additional experience to point to another type of work. For example, someone working as a Brownie leader might decide to make a change into a teaching assistant job in a primary school, or caring voluntary experience could lead to support worker or care assistant work in social care jobs. Invariably people think that voluntary experience does not count, because it is unpaid work, but job adverts that ask for, say, caring experience, do not preclude unpaid work experience. It is often the case that voluntary work, of any kind, shows commitment and dedication and impresses employers.

I'll finish with a rather typical quick-change story from my own experience. I was in a job that seemed OK but I needed some greater earning power, so while scanning the job adverts I came across one of those that is hard to resist. It looked something like this:

> Want to be earning £30,000 a year,
> working flexible hours to suit your circumstances?
> Do you have counselling or listening skills?
> Do you want to work with
> people?

Perhaps it was naïve of me to have applied, but I phoned up and was interviewed (on the phone!) for a job as an introduction agency counsellor (dating agency!) and then invited for a formal interview. It was explained that this job was essentially 'selling' the various services of an up-market introduction agency but that counselling/listening skills were also needed. Earnings depended on what was sold, training would be given, but hours worked could be weekends or evenings according to my requirements. I went for it because I liked the flexibility, it sounded fun and I needed the money. I lasted about four months and did enjoy it. It taught me a lot about myself, I gained some sales skills and I found out what I didn't want to do. I never quite hit the earning potential, but it was an excellent quick-change experience.

Medium-cooked career change

A medium change can be used as an interim phase to give you time to work on a plan that takes you to better things. It can give you a breathing space where you are earning money, gaining skills and experience, which can propel you on to other things. It might, for example, help you to fund your study or retraining for your real career plan. You may decide to stay put in your present job or just do voluntary work while you take an evening course for a qualification that will help you gain the job of your dreams. Here are two typical medium-change examples.

CASE STUDY

Georgina had worked as a sales assistant in a department store but had decided that she wanted to work abroad as a travel representative. She started by taking the ABTAC (Association of British Travel Agents) Primary Travel Certificate through evening college study, and part way through this she gained a job in a travel agency. After completing this ABTAC course she went on to take an ABTAC overseas rep course and took Spanish conversation alongside it. A year later she started work as an overseas travel rep with a large company.

She succeeded by taking measured steps towards her goal, and because she already had people experience from her sales job. The qualifications she gained proved her commitment and motivation.

CASE STUDY

Connor had been working as a sales representative for a stationery company and wanted to work as a manager in a more marketing role. He had some basic GCSEs but nothing more than his varied work experience and belief that he could do well in the management/marketing area. He started by doing a Chartered Institute of Marketing (CIM) Certificate at a local college one evening a week, which introduced him to the theories and principles of marketing, sales and advertising. His employer sent him on a management training course at a local training centre and a year later he was offered a sales manager post. His confidence had been increased by the CIM course and he was able to suggest new sales and marketing techniques to his company.

Slow dance career change

For some people there is no rush to make a career change – they just want to know that they have started and that they are moving toward their goal. For example, degree study for a new career will take at least three years and possibly five or six; if part-time study is the only option it is likely to take at least five years, but it can be worth it! Other people, who do not wish to study for a degree, may choose a slow route simply because that fits in with their lives, their commitments and circumstances.

It is worth considering what the real benefits of studying at university degree or diploma level might be. The list below covers the most common benefits:

Benefits of degree/diploma level study

- Better career prospects – certain jobs are still only open to degree/diploma level applicants.
- Earning potential may well be greater – research shows that a higher education qualification makes it likely that you will earn more throughout your life than someone without one.
- Increased confidence gained from being capable of studying at a higher level.
- Improved career choices – more careers are open to you with this type of qualification.
- You might have some fun, make new friends, expand your own personal horizons.

In addition, mature students (that is anyone over 21!) as a whole do very well when they study; as mentioned before, their motivation and commitment mean that they make the most of the higher education experience. Let's take a look at some examples of slow career changers.

CASE STUDY

Clare had three young school-age children when she decided that she might like to study further and possibly retrain for a new career. She was happy to take five or six years so that her children would become independent of her gradually. She already had some GCSEs, so she decided to take a foundation course at a local university one evening a week; she tried out subjects like Psychology, Law and Business and found that she coped well with the research and essay writing she had to do.

She moved on to do a degree without doing A-levels as the foundation course was a university Access course. She chose to study a combined course in Sociology with Education Studies and Deaf Studies. She started off the first year by studying two evenings a week, in the second year she took daytime and evening modules and for the last two years she studied full-time during the day. As she progressed she changed her study hours and timetable with the help of course advisers to suit her own situation and childcare arrangements.

When she completed her course she worked at a local school for the deaf as a support worker and also took sign language qualifications (CACDP Stages 1 and 2 – Council for Advancement of Communication with Deaf People). When her local university advertised for learning support tutors for deaf and hard of hearing students, she applied; the job advert asked for higher education experience and CACDP Stage 2, so she was an ideal applicant. As the job was termtime only and flexible hours it was perfect for her; she was able to show her motivation for working with deaf people at her interview and she was offered the job.

Tony left school with no qualifications, but had a variety of work experiences in pub management and accounts work. He felt he had never stretched himself to his full potential and when he was made redundant at 37 he decided to take some time off to gain a degree qualification. He started on a Year 0 university Access course as a full-time student and took courses in Law, Criminology and Computing and then went on to study Law and Criminology for three years. His redundancy pay and bar work supported him while he did this. He also did some voluntary work as a prison visitor. After gaining his degree he gained a place on the trainee probation officer scheme with his regional probation service; their job advert asked for maturity, life experience and people skills, and evidence of ability to study at degree standard. He was able to use all his valuable life experience and his recent study as evidence of his suitability.

CASE STUDY

Ray had trained as a motor mechanic, gaining high-level City & Guilds qualifications, and had progressed to managing a car dealership. He was a largely self-taught manager and had good IT skills. He still enjoyed the hands-on side of mechanics and had enjoyed assisting in the training of apprentices. He decided he would like to move into work as a motor vehicle tutor at a local college or a training centre, so he took a City & Guilds Further Education Teaching Certificate over two years of study one evening a week. He started to teach a car maintenance course one evening a week after gaining this qualification, and he took a short course in NVQ assessment for motor mechanic apprentices (D32 and D33 courses).
Following this he was offered part-time work teaching motor mechanics to adults at a college, and a second part-time job assessing and training young apprentices at a training centre.

Calculated risks and when you're ready!

At the beginning of this chapter I mentioned the most common reasons for paralysis amongst those wishing to make a change of some kind. We need to turn this negative thinking round, and start by asking two questions:

1. If you knew how to make a good decision (as opposed to a wrong decision), would you make it?
2. What would have to happen for you to be ready to make a career change?

The first question is designed to uncover whether you really want to make a career change or whether you are throwing up 'not being able to decide' as a smokescreen to hide your lack of motivation or a clear goal. The second question is all about readiness – are you really ready? Some people are never going to be ready, because they set impossible conditions and criteria on any career change scenario; for example they may say: 'I can only go for this if it will cost me nothing in financial, emotional or energy terms.'

They can only see the pain and are blind to the gain. They use the obstacles as their reasons for staying put and ultimately, by avoiding making a decision, they make one anyway.

For some people, readiness is about timing; they may choose to postpone deciding but revisit their researched choices a little later. Postponement is fine if you really believe timing is a crucial factor and if you are just putting your career plan back a little, but don't let it turn into procrastination.

The best advice I can give is that you research your choices well, make a plan with a timescale that suits you and then set the plan in motion in small, medium or big steps, in slow medium or quick time. Even one small step on the path of your plan can be a giant leap!

Interim problems

Often we set off on a journey with enthusiasm and a clear goal and then the car breaks down or we take a wrong turn or lose our way completely. These are just interim problems and you need to expect, if not anticipate them. In this transitional period we need to take advantage of all the encouragement and support around us so as not to get lost. It is a good idea to share our dreams and goals with children, partners, family and friends; it may be that a friend is going through their own transition and you can offer one another mutual support. Whenever you encounter a setback you will need to go through a refocusing, realignment process; you need to be flexible enough so that if one path leads to a dead end you can retrace your steps and find another. Also be aware that the struggle itself can be exhilarating and enlightening, so roll with the punches and enjoy the fight!

It's fairly obvious by now that the choices of learning/retraining are myriad; if you take the time you will uncover the best method for you. The impulse that makes us want a change is just the trigger; at every stage of the process we feel ourselves standing up to look at what's out there (peering out of the spaceship) and we might flop backwards when we see the immensity of choice before us. We have to keep dragging ourselves to our feet to peek out again and again, until we have a clear vision. We might stumble on the way and wonder whether it is worth all the effort. Look at it this way – if someone put a gun to your head and said: 'Make a change of career or die!' Then you would probably do it, because your life depends on it.

It could be that, gun or no gun, your life really does depend on it!

6 Alternative thinking and alternative work

Work just isn't what it used to be. Everything around us tells us this, but we persist in the idea of a monogamous relationship with a job, which means we expect to do it for life. It is a reassuring dream that once you find something, a job that works for you, you have found the holy grail and life will flow smoothly on until retirement. We long for the certainty and tranquillity of this in an otherwise changing and confusing world. Work, of course, is part of this changing world and reflects the needs of the capricious global situation we live in. We all get dealt some cards; we have to know how to play them. Some people who have a bad deal seem able to rise above their poor hand; others, with a better deal, just don't know how to play or blame the shuffle.

If the first part of this book has shown you how to explore meaningful work options, it doesn't mean that once you find one that will be it. You need to be flexible enough to change, change again and then again; it may be that you throw in your cards for a while and opt out. Whatever, it is good to understand some alternative work options, so that you are ready for anything – you may be surprised at how accessible and interesting some of these alternatives can be.

Portfolio working

This means that someone does more than one job at once, perhaps two or three different part-time jobs in different companies and even some homeworking (see page 91), that make up, roughly, one full-time job. It may sound rather overwhelming, but the different jobs can dovetail perfectly. Invariably people start portfolio working without intending to; perhaps a career returner decides to take a small part-time job as a viewing agent for an estate agent. After a few months, when he is more confident, he may pick up a second contract of 16 hours in the estate agent's office; a year later he may, through contacts, be offered work as a mortgage adviser at a local building society.

There are many advantages to this kind of approach. Here are a few:

1. Part-time jobs are a gentle way into a new job area, without too much commitment.
2. Trying two or three jobs at once can be an enlightening experience. Often a less fulfilling job can be dropped and the others extended to fill the gap; this allows greater flexibility.
3. Life can be more interesting with more than one job: you have two or three sets of work colleagues; every day is different.
4. It may make you redundancy proof by developing your skills and experience in more than one area; in addition, if one job begins to look risky, you may be able to increase hours in the others.

Of course, it takes flexibility to cope with portfolio working and probably needs strong organisational skills, but it is ideal for many people who want some variety in their lives. Here are some typical examples of portfolio workers.

CASE STUDY

Dan was working full time but as a single parent found the long hours frustrating. He saw a 16-hour-a-week job offered in his company as a marketing assistant that allowed him to be home based for some of the time, so he applied. He was offered the job and, at the interview, enquired about the possibility of doing some occasional promotions work for the public relations department. The company had not thought about this type of contract but agreed to trial it. Dan found that he was called upon for promotions work, which was paid at a higher rate, for about ten hours a month on average. On his non-working days he marketed himself to other employers to do the same kind of promotions work on the strength of this experience. Within a year he was working the same full time hours as previously, but as a semi-self-employed/contractually based person for half-time hours and as an employee the rest of the time.

This kind of fluid working contract is becoming quite common, and for those who are genuinely flexible and open to this kind of alternative working pattern it can work very well. It does often depend on self-marketing, 'as and when' working and some home-based working, all of which are covered in later sections of this chapter.

CASE STUDY

Gemma had highly developed skills as a jewellery assessor; she also had a qualification in jewellery making. Originally her job as a jewellery assessor was full time, while she made jewellery in her spare time and sold it at occasional craft fairs. She wanted to develop her jewellery making business further, so she reduced her hours as an assessor, spent one day a week making more jewellery and another day at craft fairs. She then approached a local college, which offered weekend leisure/hobby courses, and offered to run a half-day jewellery making course; this was a great success so she was offered an evening slot as well. She decided to take a Further Education Teaching City & Guilds course to give her a qualification in teaching jewellery making; she did this one day a week over two years. Following this, she was offered a half-time post in teaching, which she accepted, she creates jewellery the rest of the time.

This kind of work pattern has a different rhythm and flow to it than traditional working – as one job increases so another might decrease, but all according to the individual's interests and goals. It doesn't only work in creative areas, though.

CASE STUDY

Liam had worked as an accountancy technician for one company for ten years; he wanted to experience self-employment but was not sure whether this would work for him. He volunteered as a bookkeeper for a local hospice to see if he liked working on his own initiative, and found it very satisfying. With references from his voluntary employer, he approached several large charitable organisations and marketed himself for paid work on the finance or bookkeeping side. He explained that he was happy to be employed for a few hours per week for each charity, and arranged to work at five different charities on five different days a week.

Typically, portfolio working can give you a sense of freedom and exhilaration; you become multi-skilled and self-directing. It can be confusing, with a 'If it's Monday, I'm doing this; if it's Tuesday then I'm doing this' feel to it but, for those who suit it, it gives this kind of work pattern an interesting edge. Give it some consideration, as this is a developing area and is likely to be an increasingly common work system for the future.

Self-employment

This can mean many things, but it is simply another way of 'taking your life in your hands', with all the power and risks that the phrase suggests. In the new millennium the self-employment option is far more likely to mean that you have something unique to offer by way of a service, skill or talent, and that you sell that to whoever wants or needs it. It may be freelance work or consultancy based work, or a group of contracts that you service.

The key here is to focus on the word 'self'. Without a personal skills audit of the 'you' that you can be in a number of different situations, and without a clear idea of your own uniqueness, self-employment is a high-risk business. You will need to evaluate every aspect of your life, from work to leisure, hobbies, skills, talents and experience, and assess what your selling points are, and whether you can create a marketable commodity or service.

You will need to understand marketing, because you will be selling yourself. You will also need to research the potential market, and you may even have to take the time to improve your presentation skills or qualifications to be a more credible package. You may have to repackage yourself in some way, perhaps starting off in a small way doing something in your spare time and relaunching when you are sure it can take off. It may lead to mega-bucks self-employment or just something that works well for you and pays you enough.

Here are some examples.

CASE STUDY

Cameron had a good job in an investment company but found it stultifying because it was not using his main talents, which were his ability to motivate young people and his love of and talent for sport. He had the idea of offering parents a party formula of football coaching parties. He had an FA coaching qualification and a sports degree. He developed a two-hour programme that involved him teaching football skills in a fun way, with rewards and a mini-tournament in the last half-hour. The host parent would pay Cameron a set rate per child and would provide the party tea. This appealed to parents as the children had used up their energy and were ready for food! There was a small outlay for goal posts and other equipment. He started by doing parties at weekends, and although his advertising was minimal he gained bookings by word of mouth. Once he had developed the concept he approached local leisure centres to offer a party football service, which they could contract him to deliver. Bookings took off and he gave up his main job; the business was regular enough to employ some friends to do the same programme at weekends and currently he is marketing after-school football clubs along the same lines to local schools.

This is a fairly typical small undertaking based on a good idea and a clear knowledge of self.

CASE STUDY

Stephanie had not done well at school and had worked in fairly mind-numbing jobs, but at weekends she helped a family friend build and repair computers. She became quite skilled at this, so she decided to do an evening computer installation and repair qualification. She started to advertise locally to people who had PCs at home that had just gone out of guarantee, and gained a list of regular customers at the weekends. Finally, the work took off and she decided to become self-employed.

This shows how a particular talent can be used to give a chance of self-employment and be the way out of a bad work experience.

There are some very good sources of help for people considering self-employment, including the Tax Office (Inland Revenue) and Business Link (a self-employment advisory service) – see Chapter 9.

Freelance/'as and when' and consultancy work

There are benefits to employers in employing people on a freelance basis, as it helps with their cash flow, and means that their commitment to you is only 'as and when' they need you. There are even jobs advertised where this type of work pattern is on offer – a recent advert for a regional ambulance service asked for 'Casual as and when ambulance persons'. It can be relief work on quite a regular basis or very irregular, but it could be just one of a portfolio of freelance jobs that make up an interesting whole. For some early retired people it can be a useful additional income.

Again with this type of work you need to analyse your skills and talents and their marketability, do some detailed market research on who might be prepared to pay for that package of 'you' and find out what the going rate for the work might be. Obviously, if the rate you decide on represents good value to an employer, then they will be prepared to use you on a freelance basis. It is worth noting that you may be applying for work in areas where freelance is usual, or you may be proactively marketing yourself to employers who have not used a freelance before. In the latter case, a pro bono or free trial piece of work may be beneficial in selling your service.

Consultancy work is similar to freelance, but is often contracted on the basis of an acknowledged expertise in a particular area. If you do not have such expertise you may have to develop it, and a reputation, before you can operate as a consultant; but it is possible to cultivate consultancy work, while in employment, by becoming a specialist or expert. Networking and use of personal contacts are vital for prospective consultants, but employers generally want to see some tangible proof that you, as a consultant, will make life easier for them, or make money for them! This can be highly remunerative work, with management and financial consultants hiring themselves out at around £2000 a day or more.

With freelance and consultancy work it is vital to have a package of specialist qualifications, experience and fond references from major organisations in your marketing literature. It is common for freelance or consultancy workers to group together in networks or small partnerships/clusters to market themselves and offer flexibility of services. Currently, the use of the Internet can be crucial in such marketing (see page 94).

Homeworking/teleworking

Homeworking used to conjure up images of hard-pressed workers licking envelopes or schoolwork that we never wanted to do. While there are many people still involved in routine homeworking, paid at quite a low rate, it is now the case that, with PCs and the Internet in many homes, homeworking is possible in almost every job area. 'Knowledge homeworkers', doing professional jobs in IT, public relations or accountancy, can enjoy a good earning power.

Research by Leicester University shows homeworking is growing in popularity – it has more than doubled in the last 15 years. Now, more than one in four workers work for some or all of their time from home; it is predicted that by the year 2010 half of working people will be doing some of their work from home. Large organisations are realising the benefits of allowing staff to work from home, mostly through computer access with occasional visits to the workplace. Staff have proved to be more effective, more focused and more willing to offer loyalty to an employer that offers this more flexible kind of work pattern.

'Hotdesking', where home workers use office-based facilities on certain days, means that employers can maximise office space and save on large office rents. Teleworking or working using the Internet can mean you do a vast range of jobs from home, including writing, secretarial work, public relations, teaching/tutor work, accountancy, customer adviser work, travel services etc. All that is needed are good computer skills, self-discipline and somewhere quiet to work, a good PC with a fast modem and an Internet link. It may be that you do homeworking as a self-employment, freelance or consultancy option, or working for an employer. It is worth being proactive about the possibility of homeworking and suggesting it to an employer if you think it could work for you and you can make them believe it can work for them. (See 'Proactive job search' on page 96.)

Voluntary work

This has been covered before, but is worth mentioning again, as it may be the most viable option for all kinds of people. Whether it is used as an interim phase, to try out a job area or to gain qualifications and skills, it can transform people's lives by allowing them to view themselves in a different work frame, which is a valuable confidence boost and can launch new career directions or satisfying life choices. It is not fair to see voluntary work as just a means to an end, although for some people it might be, because it can be an end in itself for people not ready for, or interested in paid work. It is often the case that someone has settled for a 'day job' that pays the bills, but finds their life enhanced by something they do as a volunteer.

Here are some real examples of the benefits of voluntary work.

CASE STUDY

Philip was a new graduate with a social sciences degree and no clear career goals. He enrolled as a volunteer with CSV (Community Service Volunteers) Media and became involved in a variety of projects including radio help desk work, research for radio campaigns and basic clerical tasks. He found he enjoyed the buzz of the work and became involved in training other volunteers in the use of computers. As a volunteer, he was offered NVQ training in Community Media. After a year he gained a paid job as a trainer of volunteers.

CASE STUDY

Diane applied for voluntary advocacy training with mental health patients. Full training was given, plus expenses; she found the work, which she did for four hours a week, challenging and interesting. Two years later she gained paid work as an advocacy co-ordinator with responsibility for recruiting and training volunteers.

CASE STUDY

Jim was made redundant at 50 and wanted a change from a manufacturing environment. He had strong practical skills so offered himself as a volunteer at a training school for adults with learning disabilities, where he was a workshop instructor. He did this for ten hours a week and gained employment at the same school as a handyman/caretaker.

Anyone can do voluntary work, and contacting your local Council for Voluntary Service to discover the range of opportunities open to you will be worth the effort. Volunteers can opt to work according to their circumstances, and a disability, ill health or age is unlikely to prevent you from finding something.

Part-time work and job share opportunities

As mentioned in the section on portfolio working, part-time work can be perfect for some people, and can be done on its own or alongside something else. Quite often interesting jobs, such as speech therapy assistant, are offered on a part-time basis, and they can be very fulfilling. Other jobs, such as community playbus worker (a bus that goes out into communities), and a variety of customer service adviser jobs can offer part-time hours. Discover these by careful scanning of job adverts in local and regional papers, at job centres and recruitment agencies. Adverts usually stress life experience and maturity rather than high-level qualifications.

It is always worth considering applying for a full-time job and then asking to job share it. If you have a friend or colleague who is keen to be a job share partner you can apply for one job together or, if you can only manage a half working week, apply for it anyway. The employer may be happy to find another applicant who wants the other half. Banks and building societies and other organisations, which are anxious to retain the skills of employees, are often willing to offer job sharing arrangements, so be proactive and ask for this if it suits your circumstances.

Term-time only jobs

For many with parenting responsibilities, term-time only work is the only viable solution. Most people think that only trained teachers have the luxury of term-time only contracts, but there are many more employment options where this is possible:

- University and college teachers, tutors and instructors
- University staff in libraries, cleaning, catering, campus management, caretaking
- University and college administrative staff
- Technical staff in universities, colleges and schools, eg lab technicians, reprographics assistants, computer technicians and support staff
- School photographers
- School nurses
- Careers advisers
- Nursery nurses, non-teaching assistants, special support assistants in schools
- Catering staff in schools and colleges

- Exam invigilators
- Publishing sales representatives.

It is worth looking at a few of these in detail. It is clear that most of them are education related, and it makes economic sense for these employers to offer term-time only contracts. Some of the jobs, though education related, are offered by employers outside the educational sector.

Being a school photographer means being employed by a firm that contracts to do school/class/individual pupil photographs. An ability to get on with children plus photographic training is needed, but training is normally provided.

A publishing sales representative is mainly home-based, with visits to schools to sell publishers' educational lines. It involves presentations to staff and parents, setting up exhibitions and holding meetings with key staff members. It is a good job for an outgoing person with sales experience and an understanding of schools.

Exam invigilation is seasonal, term-time only work and requires concentration and attention to detail in supervising exams. Maturity, ability to take responsibility and calmness are required.

It is again worth being proactive if you need a term-time only contract; if you can explain the benefits to the employer they may trial it. The employer gains by recruiting someone who is available for over two-thirds of the year, more cheaply; if this fits in with their busy and quiet periods it might work out well for them.

Internet-based working

Many people are finding the Internet a source of business prospects, whether through recruitment, freelance and consultancy agencies that advertise on the net or by creating their own website and advertising their services. There are many good short courses on the Internet at local colleges and these are recommended because, once you have the basics, you will feel confident to use it to its full potential. There are also website design courses. The Internet is an enormous resource of information that you cannot afford to miss out on. It is especially useful if you need obscure information, but you need to know how to use it properly, which is why short courses can be useful. Recently I was able to find boatbuilding courses in Canada for a client of mine – he was really impressed! See Chapter 10 for more about this.

Unusual jobs and courses

The Internet can be a good resource for information on unusual jobs and courses, such as how to become a private detective or a beekeeper, but it is also possible to find them advertised in local, regional and national newspapers. Here is a sample:

- **Part–time court ushers** (18 hours per week) in a local magistrates' court. No particular experience was specified, but education to GCSE standard was required.
- **Free courses in:**
  - Welding
  - Classic vehicle restoration
  - Computer-aided draughting
  - Website design
  - Landscape design
  - Arboriculture (tree surgery).
- **Part–time tutors** wanted for courses from Aromatherapy to Zen Philosophy.
- **Radiotherapy assistant.** A friendly, caring person with good communication skills and ability to be on feet all day. Working to support professionals delivering radiation treatment. (No other qualifications or requirements specified.)
- **LGV driving or PCV** (passenger carrying vehicle) driving courses. 16–22 weeks long, offered by adult training centre.
- **Communication support notetakers** for deaf and hard of hearing students. Sign language qualification preferred.
- **Part–time cardiographer.** Working in cardiology department, an enthusiastic, self-motivated person is required to join cardiography team. Duties to include carrying out non-invasive diagnostic tests in the unit and on the wards. Experience is not essential, as full training will be given. (No qualifications were specified but a calm, confident nature and a caring disposition were required.)
- **Tailor/tailoress or dressmaker.** To assist in making customised pressure therapy garments for burns patients.
- **Trainee perfusionist** to work in a team, performing vital open heart surgery. Training will be provided for you to operate the heart/lung bypass machine and prepare heart valves for surgical implantation. A course by block release for a degree in Perfusion Science will be provided.

- **Conservation trainee** with the National Trust. Trainees needed to undertake conservation at National Trust properties across the UK. Great competition for places on this scheme.
- **Lip-reading/speech-reading course** to teach adults with acquired deafness to communicate by lip-reading.

Proactive job search

Perhaps as a child you were sent with a list to the corner shop. Supermarkets today have a range of goods not available in the past, so our current shopping list is quite different. Many of us who are trying to find work or a new career direction are using methods that are so out of date it would be like using that old shopping list in a modern supermarket. The range of options is greater – choice is king. In the corner shop we would wait in a queue to be served; in the supermarket we have to find what we want. We have to be proactive, and sometimes the demand of the consumer is strong enough to create new products or services. In the same way, if we know what we want jobwise, we sometimes have to ask for it.

Asking for it

Self-assessment and self-knowledge, that is, knowing who you are, what you have to offer and what your selling points are, are the foundations for a strong negotiating position. The next step is to determine what kind of work pattern will be suitable for you and explore who may be able to offer it. See what employers say about themselves in their adverts, on the Internet and in their promotional material. Some make statements such as 'Flexible working arrangements considered' or 'Job share possible' in their adverts. In most cases, I would recommend waiting until the offer of a job is on the table before negotiating terms. A gentle approach could be:

> *'I am really pleased to be offered the job but would be interested in doing this on a term-time only basis. How would you view this?'*

Another, more direct approach might be:

> *'I'm keen to do the job but I need a job share contract. I could do this on a trial basis, if this suited you.'*

Some people prefer to show their cards a little earlier in the selection process and may choose to mention their desire for a job share or flexible working arrangement in their covering letter. In general, you are on stronger ground once a job offer has been made and they have decided they want you. It is a sign of a good employer that they are willing to look at alternative working patterns; it probably means they are progressive and forward thinking.

Finding a good employer

This is almost as hard as finding the perfect partner in life, but if you reverse the selection process you will probably have a better chance. Employers normally start by asking if anyone they know, knows someone who can do the job. So *you* can start by asking your network of friends, family, colleagues, to find out about different employers.

Next an employer might think of using a specialist recruitment agency. You could register at some recruitment agencies and gain information from them about their employer-clients.

Or an employer might check Internet recruitment sites that have CVs of applicants. So you might look at the employer's website and see what it says about the employer.

Finally, an employer might use a job advert to attract applicants, so you could assess what the job advert says about the employer. Look for the overt message as well as the covert messages behind the words and structure of the advert.

Everything you learn from this process will help you gauge the suitability of this employer for you. Putting employers through your own selection process may create a list of good employers you want to work for. Once this is done, you can decide whether to apply speculatively or wait for them to advertise. By doing things this way you are taking control, believing in your own value and actually devising your own job search strategy. You may have been looking for work before; now, you will be looking for work in a different way. You will be playing a percentage game where you don't just let them know you are a good player, you win on points!

The age thing

Some people simply do not consider their age as being a meaningful measure of what they can or cannot do. They know their value and realise it is derived from who they are, what they can do and their skills and experience; it is not their age that counts, it is what they have done with their time. They are not particularly vulnerable to sleights and hidden comments about age, because they do not think of themselves as 'old'; they think of themselves as still 'new', because they are constantly changing, adapting and learning. These people possess a kind of wonderful madness, which manifests itself in a variety of ways – they are exhilarated by life; they fill their time to the brim.

To some people, this kind of madness is suspect and irrational. They believe that being rational is 'acting your age' and accepting other people's views of what you can and cannot do. You need to decide whether acting your age is for you. Think about whether you want someone else to write a script for you to act out, or whether you will write your own script – or even throw out the script and do some method acting, where you devise your character as you go along.

Ageist agendas

Rationally speaking, you may feel 'new' and ready for anything but, inevitably, you will come into contact with various ageist myths. Ageism is not just about prejudices towards older people; it can affect younger people, too. Age is used as a selection and recruitment sifter, although in some countries age cannot legally be used as a reason for excluding someone from a job. In the UK, however, although many employers maintain that they are flexible about age, it can still be an issue. Knowing this does not mean you have to accept it. Understanding what is behind the common myths of ageism can help you to market yourself in the right way.

Myth 1 – Older applicants will be reluctant/unable to learn new skills

We know people of all ages who believe that they cannot learn any more – they have a mental block about learning or are afraid to try. However, the explosion of courses and training available and the numbers of people going back into learning and emerging with successful achievements is proof that this cannot be true. Employers need people who are willing to learn and are afraid of taking on an older person who may be unable to cope with learning or retraining. If you can show, on your CV or application form, that you are keen to retrain or update your skills, and even say this at an interview, then you will smooth away any fears they may have. A good way to convey this is by saying or writing:

> *'I am keen to learn and develop new skills and have proved by my*
> *recent study for a basic computer course [or other example of a course*
> *undertaken] that I am a quick and effective learner.'*

By doing this you are making a positive of your willingness to learn and giving proof of this ability.

Myth 2 – Too inexperienced to do the job

Younger and older people can be accused of this; it is still about recruiters' fears that someone will not be able to learn a new skill or will take too much time to learn it. Again, being able to make a strong case for being willing to learn and being a quick learner can solve this problem. In addition, mention of how transferable your skills can be from another job will deal with the accusation of lack of experience.

Myth 3 – Too expensive to employ

Many employers think that to take on an older or more experienced person will mean greater wage costs, so they eliminate an age group to avoid this problem. It may be that you need to indicate an expected salary range in an application or, if you have been a high earner previously, suggest a lower salary expectation in a covering letter, sent with an application form or CV. For example, someone who has taken early retirement and has a pension might consider a lower salary. Similarly, it may be worth offering to work for a lower salary for a trial period, so that an employer can see your worth in real terms.

Myth 4 – Too grey/wrinkly to fit in

You may take exception to judgements being made on personal appearance – especially if you are grey and wrinkly! But, of course, appearances of any kind can influence all of us, and we can make the most bizarre assumptions based on them. Most good employers realise that a balance of ages of staff makes for a good working environment, but there are still employers who, for various sound (and unsound) reasons, place age restrictions on applicants. You will have to decide how much you want a particular area of work, and whether it is worth helping an employer to consider older employees, despite grey hairs and wrinkles. In this situation, engineering a face-to-face contact is vital so that they can get the chance to see beyond any externals to the lively young-hearted person you are. If you are not lively or young hearted you may want to consider why not! A rethink about your appearance, hairstyle, clothes etc with the help of a discerning friend may also help in how you present yourself to an employer. It is worth selling the positive reasons for employing you to an employer – perhaps people might feel more comfortable with you or you may have a consistent and reliable work record.

Myth 5 – Too old to take orders

Employers may wonder whether an older applicant might find it difficult to have a younger manager directing them or whether they might object to 'taking orders'. Mature applicants for jobs need to convey that they are happy to work under supervision or on their own initiative and can write this type of phrase on application forms or CVs. An example might be:

> 'In my work experience so far I have proved that I can work with minimum supervision, take responsibility if necessary, work under pressure and to deadlines and use my own initiative.'

Finally, it is clear that mature applicants or younger applicants may be sifted out for a reason as arbitrary as their age on an application form. If this happens regularly, and you have shown you matched the job perfectly in every way, then you need to increase the odds of an interview to better illustrate your suitability. One way to do this is to ask for some feedback if you are not shortlisted for an interview for a job you know you are suited to. This involves phoning the employer and speaking to the person in charge of recruitment. Here's an example.

Katie applied for a job but did not receive an offer of an interview. She phoned the recruiter and said:

> '*I was very interested in the job for X and was disappointed at not being shortlisted for interview. It would be a great help if you could give me any feedback about my application so that I might improve future applications.*'

The employer explained that they were inundated with applications and that they had sifted the applications on both the essential and desirable criteria for the job. Katie had matched the essential criteria as provided in the job description, but had not been as strong an applicant from the desirable criteria point of view. In addition, the employer mentioned that Katie's enthusiasm for the job had not come across in her covering letter. Katie assured the employer that it was a job she was keen to do and, in the ensuing conversation, it was suggested that she apply for a temporary position that had yet to be advertised. Katie asked if she could take the temporary position on a trial basis, thus saving the employer advertising costs. The employer agreed.

Asking for feedback about a failed application takes courage, but can often help you discover the real reason for rejection, or indeed lead to other job possibilities. In this case Katie, a career returner, had assumed that the reason for rejection was her age or lack of current work experience, whereas other factors such as lack of enthusiasm and proof of desirable qualities, as requested in the job description, were the real reasons. Too often older applicants assume that age is a rejection factor when it isn't!

In general, asking for feedback can be illuminating and useful, and shows great self-confidence and self-worth to the employer.

Let's now take an in-depth look at jobs in four categories: the ones where maturity is considered an advantage; the ones where there is no upper age limit; those where mature entry might be possible and, lastly, where there are real age restrictions or difficulties for entry.

Mature applicants encouraged/welcomed (but check individual entry requirements for qualifications)

Beauty therapy	A possible career change option that encourages mature applicants.
Bus/coach driving	There is a shortage of passenger carrying vehicle (PCV) drivers nationally, so many companies are offering free training and are welcoming the over 50s.

continued

Care assistant or support worker	Similar to social work; mature workers are the norm.
Careers adviser	Mature applicants for training are positively encouraged.
Chartered secretary	The level and type of administrative, legal and financial work in a company undertaken by a chartered secretary presupposes some life and work experience and so maturity can be a distinct advantage.
Community interpreting/ translation work	Mature people are recruited for work as interpreters/translators to help those with ethnic or community languages communicate in the courts system, gain access to government services and for translation of public leaflets etc. An ability to speak one or more community languages fluently is essential.
Funeral director	The demands of this job and the people skills required make this a likely mature person's job, despite or even because of the rather sad environment.
Guide dogs for the blind trainer	Older applicants are encouraged for this rewarding work.
Health service manager	Running the health service or a hospital department can be challenging work and so maturity and life experience can be useful.
Hospitality/pub/bar work	Life experience is important for people in this type of work.
Landscape architecture	Older applicants are encouraged to apply for degree courses.
Local government jobs	These can be jobs in a number of areas, but essentially local government (your local county, borough or city council) welcomes applications from people of all ages. Equal opportunity policies apply, and so applicants will be shortlisted for interview on the basis of a strict matching to the job requirements, regardless of age.

continued

Medical records clerk	Similar to health service manager, as ability to deal with all kinds of people and pay attention to detail is more than likely a characteristic of a mature person.
Occupational therapy	A great hands-on, caring job, which is perfect for mature people; mature trainees are welcomed.
Physiotherapist	Tough competition for places on training courses, but applications from mature people with relevant life experience are strongly encouraged.
Probation work	New training for probation officers requires applicants to have considerable life experience, so mature applicants are positively encouraged.
Radiographer	This is not as popular as physiotherapy but offers training in a caring, analytical career that can be ideal for mature entrants, who are strongly welcomed.
Retail assistant	Some retail chains deliberately recruit staff over 50.
Social work	The minimum age for qualification for social work is 22 years but, in practice, social work is often a second career and experience of life and work is highly valued.
Technical writing/authorship	A common career route for ex-engineers and one that encourages mature applicants.
Training officer	This could be in a human resources department or in a training organisation funded by the government, and mature applicants are encouraged; many have a background in another job area or have a vocational qualification.
Youth and community work	All ages are welcome for this kind of work but many youth workers are over 30; a young spirit, life experience and interest in young people are vital.

No upper age limit

Here's a list of jobs with no upper age limit for entry; see additional information for those marked *.

Archaeology – degree level study required

Banking

Barrister – degree level and postgraduate study required

Cabinet making/upholsterer/french polisher – adult short courses available at local colleges

Call centre work *

Civil service

Clerical/administrative work

Consumer protection

Court usher

Customer service work – a good area for mature people

Dental hygienist

Dental nurse

Dispensing optician – degree level study required

Environmental health

Fire service – physical fitness test is at a very high level

Further education teaching *

Health care assistant

Human resource/personnel work

Insurance

Journalism

Librarian/information management – degree level study necessary

Medical technical officer – on the job training possible

Museum curator – degree level study and voluntary work in museums would help to gain this

Nursery nursing

Optometrist – degree level study essential

Optical assistant – job adverts encourage mature applicants

Pharmacist – degree level study essential

Pharmacy technician

continued

continued

Photography

Prison governor – in practice, those under 45 are preferred

Psychology – degree level study required

Publishing – strong competition for entry to this career

Secretarial work

Solicitor – degree level study required

Speech therapist – degree level study required

Teacher training *

University lecturing *

Voluntary help management – organising volunteers for a charity

Call centre work

You have probably dealt with a call centre for financial, travel, retail or utilities services. It is worth noting that more people are employed in Britain in call centres now than in manufacturing cars and electrical goods; this figure is on the increase and expected to double in five years. The work can offer flexible working hours and opportunities for mature workers who may be able to use good communication skills and life experience to deal with a variety of customers over the phone. Unfortunately wages are low, averaging £10,500 per year, but it is a growth market for jobs, which need not discriminate on grounds of age, so may be worth considering. Some colleges are now offering short courses on call centre techniques.

Further education (FE) teaching

There are two main City & Guilds courses available at most colleges that can help people to qualify for teaching both academic and vocational subjects in further education colleges to adults, or possibly 16-to-19 year olds. They take one to two years and can be studied part time, often one evening a week. Applicants need either a degree or vocational qualifications in the subject they want to teach. For example, if someone had been a practising solicitor for a few years and wanted to teach law in a college, they could use their law degree and experience to qualify for entry to the FE teaching certificate, and run a parallel career in college teaching or launch a new one. Someone who had vocational qualifications in hairdressing or joinery could similarly take the course and train to teach hairdressing or woodwork in a college.

Most other teacher training courses need to be studied full time, for example Post Graduate Certificates of Education (PGCE) and degree courses, so the City & Guilds course can work well for people who want to keep working, and earning, while they retrain.

Teacher training

Teacher training courses for school-based work can typically take three to four years of study, at least, and although there is no upper age limit for teaching jobs in some cases it can be cheaper for headteachers to employ younger teachers. Some headteachers like to employ a mix of ages on the staff, and would employ older applicants, especially if they offered a shortage subject and/or if they could offer additional activities like running a drama, computer or football club and had qualifications in these areas. It might be wise to calculate whether you would be able to offer at least ten years teaching after qualification and, if you could, it would certainly be worth going for training. If this would not be the case, then check with your local education department and teacher training institutions before you make your decision.

University lecturing

This can be an appealing option, but prospective applicants need to have at least a first-class Honours or 2:1 degree and probably some kind of postgraduate qualification. Students studying for Masters diplomas or PhDs may be offered part-time tutorial work, which might lead into lecturing. Some lecturers these days have a teaching qualification in addition to their academic qualifications – this might be a specialist PGCE or an ordinary PGCE.

Career/job areas for mature people (many entrants are mature)

Catering – hotels/restaurants may prefer under 30 year olds; schools and hospitals would take over 30 year olds
Chiropody
Complementary medicine, including aromatherapy, homeopathy, herbal medicine, reflexology – a variety of university, college and private courses available now
Dietician
Employment/recruitment agency work
Fashion designer – design area often favours younger people

continued

Graphic designer – as with Fashion designer

Hairdressing – many mature hairdressers do self-employed, mobile work

Holiday representative – a small trend in companies specialising in holidays for older people to recruit mature holiday reps – see Overseas travel representatives on page 109

Illustrator – as with Fashion designer

Interior designer – growth area in courses due to TV programmes; some options for self-employment

Legal executive

Media/film/TV work – some indication that youth is favoured!

Midwifery – most entrants to midwifery are over 21 years; it may be difficult to train over the age of 50

Nursing – some schools of nursing may have an upper age limit of 45 years for entering training

Police – some forces may consider applicants in their 40s

Purchasing officer – Chartered Institute of Purchasing and Supply courses available through evening study at various colleges

Security work – most companies want mature applicants between 21 and 45 years; some take people up to the age of 60

Sports and leisure management

Sports coaching

Surveying

Textile designer – as with Fashion designer

Town planning

Traffic warden – some areas have a maximum age limit of 55 years; others take people up to retirement age

Translator

Age restrictions or job areas where entry is difficult for mature people

Acting – it may be difficult to enter the acting profession over the age of 30

Advertising – large proportion of agency staff in 30s and up to 40

Ambulance work – age range of 18 to 55 years, but for paramedic/ technician training this might reduce to an upper age limit of 40

Computer jobs – employers have different attitudes to mature applicants

Dental technician – most trainees are under 30 years

continued

> Dentist – most dental schools take applicants up to the age of 30 – check with individual schools
>
> Hotel management – some hotel group training schemes have an upper age limit of 25 to 30 years
>
> Licensed pub management – trainees tend to be between 25 and 50
>
> Marketing – mostly 25 to 35 year olds
>
> Medicine - most medical schools take applicants up to the age of 30 – check with individual schools
>
> Retail manager – some trainee schemes may have a maximum upper age limit of 35 years
>
> RSPCA inspector – maximum age of entry is normally 40 years
>
> Veterinary science – only a few mature entrants to veterinary school each year

Within all of these four categories there will be exceptions, so please use these lists as guidelines, and if you see your dream job in any category check carefully before you make your plans.

You might find it interesting to consider the following jobs, which were advertised with mature applicants in mind.

Part-time tutors

The Workers Educational Association and local colleges often advertise for tutors with proven qualifications and/or expertise in a range of subjects to teach leisure/hobby or qualification based classes; so if you have a skill or hobby, you may be able to teach it.

Telesales for Insurance companies

A major insurance company has advertised recently for staff to be trained for telesales and specified 'third age career returners' in their advert. 'Third age' generally refers to people in the later parts of their working lives. The company wanted positive, articulate, hard-working people with good listening skills to contact people by phone to arrange appointments for insurance advisers.

Hobby therapist with retired people

If you have a craft, a skill or hobby, or several, you could teach these activities to elderly people in retirement homes, residential care homes or in sheltered accommodation.

Museum assistant

Paid and volunteer work is available in local and regional museums and is perfect for those mature people with a strong sense of history. One retired schoolteacher I know was working up to the age of 70 as a volunteer guide in a local museum.

Support workers for adults with learning disabilities

There are some ESF (European Social Fund) training schemes available for this kind of work.

Home start support worker

This is mainly voluntary work with young families who need support or a listening ear.

Driving instructor/driving examiner

If you have the patience, this might be the right kind of career change; some driving schools advertise for trainee drivers and put them through their training for a fee. It is a good way to be self-employed. The Driving Standards Agency can give information about driving examiner training.

Scuba diving instructor or other types of diving work

There are a variety of courses offered in this kind of work through the Professional Association of Diving Instructors (PADI) or Health and Safety Executive courses; some government funding may be available.

Overseas travel representatives

Airtours advertises for mature people with customer service experience and excellent interpersonal skills for their Golden Years Hosts vacancies, as they believe mature hosts are better suited to being holiday representatives for mature customers. The age range for these vacancies is 21 to 60 years, and if the idea of hard work, long hours and the winter season abroad appeals to you, then this might suit you. Airtours recruitment hotline: 01706 909027.

Some jobs that might be good to train for

Certain predictions about work in the new century are worth mentioning, and they have a lot to do with the fact that third world labour can make goods cheaper than we can in the UK, and the fact that we are all generally living longer.

The first point to be clear about is that likely growth areas for jobs will continue to be in service industries and away from manufacturing. Service industries mean any service to the public, that is leisure centres, hotels, shops, travel companies, banks, building societies, insurance companies, call centres etc. The second point is that there will continue to be growth in anything to do with old people; this could mean jobs in pensions, social care and support, health care etc.

So if you are looking for a career change it might be worth exploring these areas. In addition, it is worth looking at shortage areas for jobs as a possible career change option. Shortage areas are in jobs such as nursing and health therapies, eg physiotherapy, occupational therapy, and radiography where, once qualified, job opportunities are fairly assured, and in teaching (in particular, shortage subjects such as Maths, Sciences, Languages, Design Technology and IT). There are also predicted demands for qualified managers, surveyors and engineers in the construction industry, with vacancies on degree and HND programmes.

Some rural skills are in decline and this has caused shortages in areas such as rural metalworking (blacksmithing), dry stone walling and thatching. Some agricultural colleges can offer short courses in these and other areas, including courses in arboriculture (tree surgery), golf course management, gamekeeping and waterkeeping.

Here are a couple of examples of people who made some interesting career changes.

CASE STUDY

Matt had worked in engineering for some time as a manager but due to a back injury could no longer do desk work. He needed to be active to retain his flexibility and health. He had loved welding when he trained as a craft engineer, he had a creative side that he never used and liked designing and making things. I suggested a rural metalworking course, which was a free daytime adult course at a local college; he would learn to design and make ornamental gates, design metalwork and make horseshoes. (He would not be able to shoe horses, unless he took the Worshipful Company of Farriers apprenticeship training.) He decided on completing his course to set up business in the borders of Scotland.

CASE STUDY

Scott had been made redundant and wanted a career change that would use his love of the country and interest in gardening. I suggested he try some volunteer countryside ranger work at a local national park. At the same time he worked as a volunteer at the British Trust for Conservation Volunteers and was taught to build dry stone walls and lay paths. He took a short course in arboriculture and gained a Health and Safety Certificate, which allowed him to gain work on a contractual basis for the local council in tree surgery. When a paid countryside ranger post was advertised he beat off stiff competition and was offered the job, based on the breadth of his experience, his arboricultural qualification and his new skills.

Redundancy – the ugly word

We look for reasons for the things that happen to us, and too often leap on something that has no real basis in fact. For example, we probably know rationally that redundancy or outplacement has nothing to do with inadequate work performance but, at the back of our minds, that reason takes root and grabs us by the throat, should our turn for redundancy come round. Percentage wise these are the main reasons for redundancy in order of likelihood:

1. Reorganisation and mergers
2. Company restructuring or retrenchment due to changing market conditions
3. Closure for economic or market reasons
4. Personality clashes
5. The very smallest percentage may be due to someone's inadequate work performance.

The odds are that if you are selected for redundancy it is far more likely to be for reasons 1–4 than 5. Nonetheless, it is difficult, in the midst of shock and disappointment (often common feelings for those being made redundant), to be rational about the reasons. In my experience, there are two further points worth noting:

1. Jobs, not people, are made redundant. That is, the jobs people do become less useful or technology takes over and fewer people are needed.
2. Managers' jobs are often made redundant because it is too costly to continue paying the managers.

None of these reasons, therefore, has much to do with job performance. Interestingly, research using a psychometric test profile on redundant managers shows that as a breed they are intelligent, resourceful, self-suffi-cient and imaginative. These skills can often ease their way into new employment or self-employment, if they can survive the process with self-esteem intact. For many redundancy/outplacement can be an oppor-tunity for self-enlightenment; for others it can result in depression and the appearance of some rather obvious chips on shoulders.

The chip on shoulder syndrome

We all have these in some shape or form, unless we are incredibly enlight-ened individuals. Some of us become aware of them and can then deal with them; others have boulders rather than chips!

It is a good friend who can bring your attention to negative attitudes or chips because they can get in the way of you finding new work. So eat them, burn them, throw them, but get rid of them. If you find yourself railing against the world, blaming everyone for your situation, feeling sorry for yourself, thinking 'What's the point?', then you could be collecting chips. Dwelling on the past and past slights will not help you; moving forward in a positive way will.

The up side

On the theme of 'what doesn't kill you, makes you strong' it is worth telling yourself that the experience of redundancy has developed a new and powerful skill in you – the skill of survival. The facts may seem depressing but redundancy is a possibility for most workers in their lives; some have already experienced it two or three times. We cannot make ourselves completely redundancy proof, but we can manage our careers better (see Chapter 10) and be better equipped for the future. Here's an example of someone who, at 74, is still working today, but who at 57 years of age survived his first redundancy.

CASE STUDY
Frank had worked for one employer for over 25 years when changes in the shipping industry threatened his job and caused him to be made redundant. He had a robust self-esteem, even though this was a blow, and he needed financially to continue working. He had been grey since his 50s, but was extraordinarily fit and active, as well as being a near obsessional golfer! He did not even think of checking the job adverts, as he believed that his contacts would help him more. He networked with colleagues and contacted people over the phone, as well as sending letters 'on spec' to targeted companies. He wrote a good letter

with details of his experience and what he believed he could do to make money for these companies. He never mentioned his age in his letters, as he didn't think it was an issue and didn't want to make it one. When asked his age at an interview, he pronounced himself '57 years young' and emphasised his experience and contacts in the shipping industry. He was offered a job at his first interview, due partly to an accomplished interview performance (he was confident and marketed himself well) and partly to his extreme likeability and interpersonal skills.

Two years later he was made redundant again, but gained another job in much the same way. A year later it happened again and he gained a third job, which he worked at full time till retirement aged 65. Currently, at 74 years of age, he is still working two days a week for that last firm; he plans to reduce this to one day a week for his 75th year! This is a testament to survival and an example to us all.

It is interesting that Frank did not use a CV or standard application procedures. Had he used a CV it would have looked something like the one that follows. I have created it as an example of how concise and compelling a CV can be for an older person with good experience and personal qualities. It is a resumé, one-page style that I think works well to show the breadth of his experience, without dwelling too much on detail. It also draws less attention to his age, but emphasises his young spirit and his physical fitness (see page 114).

Mature graduates and what they can do – just about anything!

Many career changers consider degree or diploma level study in courses as varied as agriculture, social work, nursing, teaching, psychology, law and so on; invariably they find this type of study challenging and stimulating, whether they study full time, half-time or part time or through distance learning. Mature students study for a million different reasons, which might be any of the following:

- to prove they can study and gain a higher level qualification;
- to see what higher level study is like;
- to improve their future job prospects;
- to improve their earning potential;
- to train for a specific career;
- to open up possible career opportunities;
- to explore a subject that interests them. (Continued on page 115)

Older and wiser person's CV

Frank Ford
5 Sussex Gardens, Cheston
Surrey
0171 0000 00
email:fford@xxxx

An experienced logistics and distribution manager with a shipping industry background, seeking employment opportunities on a contractual/consultancy or part-time basis.

Key skills and achievements

- Strong interpersonal skills used to make contacts, liaise with international ports and customers and to maximise speed of delivery of goods and cargoes.
- Organisational skills with an ability to work to fine deadlines to eliminate costly delays of supplies to marine fleet and to prevent financial penalties for late arrival of goods and cargoes.
- Management of department of 50 employees with overall responsibility for a fleet of 45 ships, involving training and development of staff.
- Achievement of Advanced Certification through the Chartered Shipbrokers exam, undertaken by part-time study; highest grade achieved in specifications of international ports.
- Worldwide contacts with potential for future business opportunities.
- Excellent numerical skills used in all aspects of costing, financial and auditing work.

Career history

1952–84   **Brent Line Shipping Company, London**
Shipping manager with total responsibility for fleet of 45 ships, sailing to all parts of the world, with sharp cost limitations and pressurised working conditions. This required an ability to make detailed financial estimates for bidding for cargoes, management of stores for outbound ships and 'people' skills for dealing with customers and staff. The department made year on year savings and profits by careful management and good organisational systems.

1957–67   **Walker Accountants, Surbiton**
Parallel part-time work as **auditing assistant** for small local businesses, requiring strong numerical skills, attention to detail and knowledge of profit and loss accounts.

1945–52   **Taylor Gunson, Calcutta, India**
Accounts manager for large shipping supplier.

Education history

1937–1945   **Francis Xavier College**
Senior Cambridge exam taken (A-level equivalent) in 8 subjects: English, Maths, Latin, History, Geography, Science, RE and Hindustani.

Personal

I am an outgoing, sociable person and make and develop business and ordinary friendships easily. I have a reputation for being hardworking and for being an effective manager of people, along with having a good business sense. With the current reductions in the shipping industry it is vital to work harder each year to make a profit, and I have found that I can respond to these changing circumstances with a positive attitude and determination to succeed.

My interests outside work have always been sport related and in the past I competed at a high level in athletics and hockey. Currently I keep fit through golf, which is something of a passion for me. I complete The Times crossword each day in under an hour and this serves to keep my brain as fit as my body. Any other time is spent with my wonderful family.

Excellent references available on request

Changing career to change your life

Interestingly, mature students do not always go for the more obviously useful vocational subjects such as engineering, nursing, social work etc. Many mature students just pick a subject that interests them, often studying on Combined Honours or modular degree courses that allow a combination of subjects. Some might choose a major/minor combination and spend 75 per cent of their time on, say, Maths, and 25 per cent on, say, Italian ab initio. Ab initio is a subject taken from scratch with no prior knowledge, and this often appeals to mature students. Alternatively, students might take a joint degree where equal time is spent on two subjects.

Some students are loath to take a general subject degree, as opposed to a vocational one, because they see it as less useful. However, the facts show that graduate recruiters are often happy to take on someone with a general degree, and that many graduate vacancies are for those with any degree. Many recruiters have to offer specialist training, so that the degree subject is less important than what degree level study proves you can do, which is that you can:

- self-motivate/work on your own initiative;
- learn new skills;
- research and analyse information;
- write in an articulate way;
- present information by way of formal presentations;
- work on team projects.

In terms of future job prospects it has been proven that, in general, graduates earn more in their working lives than the non-graduate working population (see page 119), but a degree does not guarantee a great career, unless you plan your career strategy in a measured way. A clear career goal and strong self-knowledge will be needed for any graduate, but mature graduates have restrictions due to family commitments and geographical limitations, which mean that they have to be more focused and motivated to gain the career they desire.

AGR (Association of Graduate Recruiters) carried out a survey in 1999 of 'Activity in the graduate labour market', which found that there was an increase in graduate vacancies in IT, science and engineering, marketing and sales. Vacancies in the small and medium-sized companies showed an increase, which could be good news for mature graduates not able to access the big employers due to geographical limitations. The Internet was also playing a part in graduate recruitment and 64 per cent of graduate careers services now publish graduate vacancies on the Internet.

Any mature student needs to use the facilities of his/her local university or college careers service as local and regional employers use them to advertise their jobs.

What is a graduate job, anyway?

There are two answers to this question: it could be specifically identified graduate-level training that requested a degree in the advert; or it could be any job a graduate chooses to do. Many graduates need to start in a below degree-level vacancy to develop work skills to support their academic skills; this might seem like a backward step, but the willingness to start a little lower impresses employers, who might otherwise criticise graduates for lack of experience. Once in a work situation graduates can progress to better opportunities with their valuable skills.

What can mature graduates do?

They can do anything and everything, as long as they are persistent, motivated and willing to keep on learning.

Job search tips for older and wiser people

To sum up here are some key job search tips for older and wiser people:
- Decide what you mean by work (part time, full time, casual, as and when, consultancy, voluntary).
- Find or create a niche for yourself with your present employer or sell yourself and your experience to a different employer.
- After redundancy, think of promoting/marketing yourself back to an employer on a freelance basis.
- Unwrap the package that is you, discover your transferable skills, rewrap yourself in a more interesting way.
- Cultivate mentors/colleagues/contacts for future chances of work.
- Network at every opportunity.
- Use voluntary work as a way to expand experience and skills, and as a way into other jobs.

And finally, remember that age is just a number. If some employer makes it an issue, decide if you want the job enough to fight for it by proving just what an older and wiser person can do. If not, move on to another employer who has the sense to value human beings for who they are and who they have become.

Money and how to get it

Money is supposed to be a dirty word, but we need to deal with it because it can be a motivation, an obstacle, a concern, a burden. Some of us feel embarrassed to be driven by money, but for most people money plays an enormous part in their lives and cannot be ignored. It does not mean that money has to rule, but it is a necessary and serious consideration. We often subscribe to the belief that the best things in life are free, but act as if this is not true! Money is a means to an end and is as much about our own need for security, importance or power; it is rarely an end in itself.

Lack of money

This is often a motivating factor for people in low-paid jobs who need a greater earning power; it is not the best motivation, although it can be a good trigger, but it will not be a sustainable motivation without research into what else is available and what someone is suited to. Occasionally I meet someone who likes their work but is disappointed with the monetary value put on it. Often they have to choose between doing something that is meaningful for them and something that is less rewarding but pays better. Their choice depends upon their criteria for work and whether the pay aspect is important to them.

Nonetheless, lack of money in a job does not have to mean a complete change. It may mean that someone has to look for progression in their career as a way of increasing their earning power, and that might mean retraining or a return to study to gain higher qualifications. However, there is sometimes a cost to retraining that may be a further obstacle to pulling out of the low pay trap, so here are the best ways round this problem.

Low cost/nil cost ways of retraining/gaining better qualifications

Any daytime Access course under 16 hours at your local college will be free, so if you are a part-time or shift worker, or returning to work after a break, this is the best way to retrain, 'upskill' or gain new qualifications. See Chapter 5 for details. Some courses through your local TEC (Training and Enterprise Council) or LSC (Learning and Skills Council, the new government-funded agency) will be free of charge.

If you are unemployed and in receipt of benefits, on Income Support or Family Credit, if you have recently been made redundant in a large-scale redundancy, or if you have ill health or a disability, most courses at colleges and at training suppliers funded by the TEC/LSC will be free.

Free employment-based training through your current employer may be available and can lead to nationally recognised qualifications in the workplace such as NVQs, or in-company training courses can improve your career prospects, whether you stay with that employer or move on.

The average cost of courses at local colleges is about £120, with many costing £60–70, and as different types of payment plans are generally available, including direct debit, payment costs can be spread over a period. Colleges have Access funds to help students in financial difficulties and students can apply for financial help towards the cost of childcare, books, travelling to college etc.

An Individual Learning Account through your local TEC can provide you with £150 towards the cost of your study – see page 122.

For more expensive courses like Counselling level 3 (about £800–1000) or a Chartered Institute of Marketing course (about £200–300) or Association of Accounting Technicians courses (about £200–300), a Career Development Loan through your local TEC might be available, see page 122.

For degree or diploma courses at universities, student loan financing is available, see next section.

Whatever the cost there are ways to offset it, if you are prepared to explore them. In real terms, when someone says that something is too expensive, it is important to ask the question 'Compared with what?' We all find money for necessities and with careful budgeting can invariably find money for small luxuries. Perhaps you need to stop looking at retraining as a luxury and start seeing it as a necessity. Think about it this way; if an average course costs £200, compare it with ten nights at the pub or ten afternoons watching your favourite football team. Now I'm not saying that nights at the pub don't have their value but it puts the cost into perspective.

It is a problem when lack of money prevents you from improving your career prospects, when earning a living becomes the only priority and earning a living in itself stops you really living. It may be that your income is low and you have to use an Individual Learning Account as a saving plan for study or retraining; or you may have to spread out your retraining over a longer and financially more manageable period. But if you decide to go for your goals, however long it takes and however much discomfort it involves, financial or otherwise, the benefits will buoy you up – I know, I've met people who've done it!

Sources of financial help

Let's take a look at the highest level of study first. For most professional, high-earning careers, some kind of degree level study is required and this can incur two main expenses:

1. The cost of supporting yourself while you study. If you study full time you will only be able to work part time. Most students have some sort of part-time income these days, but remember that on it you will have to fund your accommodation, food, other necessities, support your family (if you have one), pay for books and materials etc. If you are studying part time you may be able to work full time, but you will still have additional study costs such as books, materials etc.

2. Most university courses charge tuition costs for each year of the course, which can be as much as £1025 (maximum tuition fee for 1999/2000). Part-time courses, which are spread over anything from four to six years, often have tuition fees per module, but the cost can be spread over a longer period; typical per module costs may be £300. Many students will not have to pay tuition fees if their financial situation is below a certain level. Your local education authority (LEA) will assess your eligibility for payment or exemption from tuition fees by a process of means testing (assessing your financial means, your income if any, whether you have parents supporting you or whether you are an independent student etc). You apply to your LEA once you have applied for a course at university and they will assess you and whether/what amount of Student Loan you will be eligible for (see page 120).

It is worth noting that all the research shows that doing a degree, even though incurring some financial cost, will certainly be of financial benefit, not just immediately after the course but throughout your life and career. The Institute of Fiscal Studies found in a survey of 40-year-old male graduates that they earned 15–20 per cent more than their peers who left school with A-levels. Female graduates' earnings were 40 per cent higher than their non-graduate peers, although still lower than their male graduate colleagues.

The system for funding university or higher education has changed drastically in the last few years, so it is important to gain accurate information about the financial support available to students from your local LEA and the Department for Education and Employment (DfEE). The DfEE produces a guide, 'Financial support for students', which is available by calling 0800 731 9133.

What student loans really are

The good news is that depending on your financial situation, the assessment by the LEA and whether you are studying in or outside London, you will be eligible for a student loan of about £2875 to £4480 per year of your course. Many students will lose about a quarter of this amount per year due to the LEA assessment, but most will get at least three-quarters of the amount to help fund their study. The average student on graduation will therefore owe between £6000 and £12,000. This seems like a heavy burden, but the repayments timetable can make it much more manageable.

You will not be expected to start paying back the loan until the April after you have finished the course; how long it takes you will depend entirely on your circumstances. You repay a percentage of your income each year until you have repaid the loan, and your instalments will be smaller if you have a low income. For example, on an income of £11,000 you will be expected to pay £7 per month, which is taken out at source by your employer. If you were to earn below £10,000 for the whole of your working life you would pay nothing, as repayments only start once your salary rises above £10,000. The percentage repayment will go up as your income rises, with for example someone earning £15,000 paying 3% (£37 per month).

Some high earners will pay back the loan quickly; others may have breaks in repayment periods and may never pay it off before retirement. *On retirement, the loan will be cancelled as long as you have kept up your repayments, according to the agreed conditions.* The amount that you pay back will be linked to inflation so that, according to the DfEE, 'the value of the amount you pay back will be broadly the same as the value of the amount you borrowed'.

There are a number of situations where you would have no repayment obligation – if you are out of work, having a parenting break, if you are too ill to work or if you die. (No one else has to repay the loan if you die.)

There are also supplementary grants available to students in particular circumstances. In addition, universities have Access funds and hardship loans for students who are in financial difficulties.

This is a very brief description of a complex subject, so I would strongly advise you to check with your local LEA and the DfEE, and read a book called *Students' Money Matters* published by Trotman for the fuller picture.

Training incentives for shortage subjects in teaching

Shortage subjects are those with a shortage of applicants for courses or a shortage of teachers of these subjects. For those with a National Curriculum subject at degree level who wish to take a Postgraduate Certificate of Education (PGCE) to train to teach Maths or Science, there are financial bursaries of £5000, offered in two parts. The first £2500 is offered on entering a PGCE Maths or Science course and the second £2500 on achieving the PGCE and taking up a teaching post in Maths or Science.

In addition, for those entering initial teacher training courses at undergraduate level for teaching degree courses in secondary shortage subjects, support is available, based on need, of up to £5000 in one year. The secondary shortage subjects are Maths, Science, Modern Foreign Languages, Design and Technology, Music, Religious Education and, for 1999/2000, Geography.

National Health Service (NHS) bursaries

NHS bursaries are available on NHS funded places for pre-registration courses in:

- Chiropody
- Dental hygiene
- Dental therapy
- Dietetics
- Nursing
- Midwifery
- Occupational therapy
- Orthoptics
- Physiotherapy
- Prosthetics and orthotics
- Radiography
- Speech and language therapy.

The NHS will pay the full tuition fee for these courses. Contact the NHS Students Grant Unit on 01253 856123.

Career Development Loans (CDL)

CDLs can help pay for education or training that will make you more employable. They are actually deferred bank loans, processed in the first place by your local TEC, and are available through three main high street banks (the APR% is variable). The DfEE pays the interest on the loan while you are studying or retraining.

You would be able to borrow between £300 and £8000, but you would make no repayments during the study or training. CDL recipients may qualify for vocational tax relief on course costs. Some TECS can give additional grants to CDL applicants of up to 10% of the approved loan (normally up to a maximum of £300). This might mean someone applies for £2000 and gains an extra £200 free of charge.

A CDL cannot be combined with an LEA award, but it can be combined with an ILA (Individual Learning Account), see below.

Individual Learning Accounts

These are instant access savings accounts, held with a bank, and designed to encourage you to invest in your own learning, training and development. You open the account by depositing £25, and the local TEC then gives you £150 free, to be spent on course fees for a range of courses at recognised colleges or training providers. You could start saving a small amount each month towards a future career move, in preparation for a time when you are ready for a change, or you could use the £150 straight away to enrol on a course. A portion of the money can often be used to pay for professional careers advice. Further incentives and discounts on eligible courses should be available from April 2000. Contact your local TEC/LSC for further information and application packs.

It is important to assess whether the money it takes to do something different will be worth it to you. There is a cost to everything, and not only in financial terms. There are benefits, too, and these need to be weighed up before making a decision. Doing nothing has its own costs too, financial and otherwise. There are a number of sources of funding, but if the worst happens and you have to do it on your own, only you will be able to decide the real value of making a change. Are you ready to spare some change to make a change?

Going to POT or people, organisations and things that can help you

People

I've mentioned some of the sources of help before, but what follows is as definitive a list as I can come up with of real people who have helped serious career changers.

The people who really love you

There are some people who can see that you are not exactly where you want to be and who know your true potential. They encourage, coax and support you and enjoy your successes with you. Sometimes working for your own goals means these other people can be burdened a little more – you may have less time for wearisome chores, which you may be glad to abandon. Unfortunately, this generally means that they have to be picked up by someone else; if that kind of someone helps you gladly, you are truly loved. The people who support you most of the time are to be prized, appreciated and rewarded. Making time to spend with these people is an important part of any career or life plan, not just for what they can do for you, but because they may decide to go for their own dreams as you have pointed the way. Fun and relaxation should be part of the plan too, otherwise you will just be a driven person.

Colleagues/mentors/role models

Similarly, these people can have a huge impact on how you realise your own potential, so pay attention to those who work around you and let them guide you, stimulate you, open you up to new possibilities. Return the courtesy by offering encouragement and recognition when they strike out for what fits with their dreams.

The proviso that comes with the above two categories of 'helpers' is that you might encounter people who purport to be on your side but who, in fact, hold you back, knock your confidence and warn you of dire happenings that will result from you making a change. See right through this and know it as a manifestation of their own thwarted lives rather than any representation of how you should progress. Be alert and vigilant to fend off their 'I warned you this would happen' remarks when things don't work out; it won't just flow smoothly, but as long as you keep on making progress and are flexible enough to take an alternative route when necessary, you will succeed.

Careers advisers/counsellors

This may seem a rather biased view, but as this is my personal calling I must recommend time spent with a careers professional as time well spent. We do help people change their lives and sometimes we can act as a trigger; at other times we can give you a push. Careers advisers spend a lot of time visiting local and national employers to find out 'what is out there' for their clients. They also know all about education, colleges and universities and can research and uncover bizarre or common courses for your delight. Most careers advisers love to help their clients make connections between who they are and what they can do best with their lives; some, like me, also like to find out about obscure courses such as worm farming, just to be an interesting guest at dinner parties!

At local careers offices or centres, run by careers companies funded by the government, you may be able to access free (to the unemployed) or subsidised (to those in paid work) careers guidance. There will probably be an up-to-date careers information library/resource where you can find information on a vast range of careers and jobs. In addition, computer-aided guidance packages will be available, which will generate career and job suggestions, matching your computer profile. Some careers centres can arrange psychometric assessment, either free of charge or for a fee, which can help you discover your real strengths and help predict useful career directions for you.

University careers services offer a similarly excellent service for university students and graduates, with professional careers guidance counsellors available.

For details of local careers centres check in the phone directory, with your local TEC (Training and Enterprise Council) or with the newer Learning and Skills Councils (LSC), a government agency combining the

FEFC (Further Education Funding Council) and the TECs. These new LSCs will be the best resource for information on all education courses and work-based or other training in your local area.

Occupational psychologists

These are skilled, highly trained psychologists who can advise on suitable careers by using scientific and psychometric (measuring your mind) tests. Consultations are on a fee basis, but it may be worth it to discover your true potential and have a psychometric test score to prove it. Many private careers consultancies advertise in the national press in recruitment sections.

Career coaches

Having a career coach is like having a careers adviser/mentor/supporter at the end of a phone line, whom you can use to help motivate you to make the changes you know you want, and who will keep an eye on your progress. A weekly chat with a career coach can put your career plan into overdrive. You hire a coach to ensure that you have the impartial, independent advice and support to take your life where you want it. A coach helps you develop your fitness for your own purposes by challenging you, listening to you, helping you set your own goals and see them through. You take the coaching process seriously because you pay for it, although it is not costly and can benefit those who procrastinate or those who just don't get around to working their lives out. Coaching can last a few weeks or months, depending on your career plan. Many coaches offer a free trial as an introduction. There is plenty of information on the Internet.

College guidance advisers

Most colleges have advisers who can help you understand the types of courses available and where they could lead. Make sure that you shop around all your local colleges, as there is great diversity amongst the courses on offer and it is fascinating to find out all the wonderful ways that you can stretch yourself. These advisers offer a free service, so use them well.

Librarians

There is a mass of useful information, in paper or computerised form, available in main, academic/university or business libraries. Strive to nurture a relationship with a friendly librarian and you will have access to a treasure trove, including company reports, professional journals and newspapers, local business news, commercial services and business directories listing companies that you may wish to target. Librarians are also a good source of information on charities, volunteering and the Internet. You may even find courses that you can study online from your local library. In general, they will be pleased to help you, as this means they can use their own expertise and prove that they are not just there to stamp books!

Disability employment advisers

These are specialist advisers based in most jobcentres (government centres where jobs are advertised) who are responsible for supporting and helping people with disabilities or health problems of any kind. They can search for vacancies that are disability friendly, recommend work suitable to an individual's situation and suggest local employers who may be worth approaching. They can also refer people for specialist free adult training, according to their needs, or for assessment to see what is the best choice of employment available.

Self-employment business advisers

These business advisers, whether based in a bank or in a business organisation, can help you create a business plan, seek out finance, market and promote yourself etc. You can bounce ideas off them and benefit from their expertise, as they have often been self-employed themselves. They will be tough with you, so that you go into self-employment with your eyes open.

Organisations

Some of the above people work in the following organisations, but it is good to know just who is out there to help you.

Business Link

This is a national network of business support services, set up by the Department of Trade and Industry for those interested in self-employment. They can also advise on the most suitable training for your needs or refer you to other specialist agencies.
Contact Business Link Signpost Line 0345 567765

Community Service Volunteers (CSV)

An organised programme of full-time volunteering for 16–35 year olds available throughout the country; volunteers are given accommodation and pocket money. This is a common starting point for those who wish to go into caring or social services.

CSV Volunteer Programme Head Office 020 7278 6601

Council for Voluntary Service/volunteer bureau

Make sure you find out about all the wonderful volunteering opportunities that are available in your area. There may be valuable training available or just the chance to develop your skills or self-confidence; you decide the time commitment, and you may get the chance to try out work that is more interesting than your paid work. For details, ask at your local library or check in the phone directory.

CSV Media

A rather interesting offshoot of CSV, offering volunteer training in social action broadcasting, support services and media training.

Contact at CSV number above

Department for Education and Employment (DfEE)

This is the government department with responsibility for all education and training; they produce useful information on a number of careers-related subjects.

Contact 020 7925 5000

Educational Grants Advisory Service

This is an independent agency for people wanting funding for further or higher education.

Telephone the Information Line on 020 7249 6636

Learn Direct

Learn Direct offers free help, advice and information on learning and careers via the telephone.

Telephone 0800 100 900

National Extension College (NEC)

The NEC is one of the leading providers of distance learning courses for A-levels, GCSEs, degrees, vocational and general interest subjects. New this year are IT courses in wordprocessing, spreadsheets and databases, a Certificate in Playwork for people working with children in out-of-school playclubs and a Business and Management degree through Anglia Polytechnic University.

Contact NEC Tel: 01223 450500; website www.nec.ac.uk

Open and Distance Learning Quality Council

This is a wonderful source of information on accredited distance learning/correspondence/flexible study courses.
Website www.odlqc.org.uk/odlqc

Open University

This has been mentioned before, and this is a highly regarded educational institution with regional bases and excellent tutorial support. Students often start on Level 1 courses, which can be in the arts, social sciences, maths, science or technology, and are a preparation for degree-level study, for those who have not studied at this level before. They would then progress to a selection of Level 2 and Level 3 courses, which have credit ratings or a points score, that build up to a degree. There are no minimum entry requirements and students can spread courses over many years with breaks in between or work at a pace to suit their circumstances.

Courses normally include study materials sent by post, video, cassette or radio or TV programmes, regular tutorial meetings at study centres in the local area and, for some, one-week residential courses. First degree and postgraduate courses are currently offered, with the majority being very academic (theory based) in content rather than strongly vocational.

A typical 60-point course can cost about £320; a degree course is made up of 360 points, so it can be costly, but so is ordinary degree-level study these days, with many students paying £3000 worth of tuition fees for an average degree course – see Chapter 8. It is possible to arrange to pay fees by instalments through an Open University student budget account, which can help spread the cost.

For general enquiries contact the Central Enquiry Service, PO Box 200, The Open University, Walton Hall, Milton Keynes MK7 6YZ; website www.open.ac.uk/frames.html

Skill: National Bureau for Students with Disabilities

A brilliant source of help for students with disabilities.
Contact 020 7450 0620

TEC Training and Enterprise Councils
(soon to be the Learning and Skills Councils LSC)

These are government-funded organisations, responsible for work-based training for young people and adults. They can advise on availability of training courses, which might be NVQs or other qualifications. They often sponsor courses in shortage areas and for minority groups such as women returners or ethnic minorities. They administer the Career

Development Loans and Individual Learning Accounts programmes (see Chapter 8). They can also advise on self-employment and may run training courses for the self-employed on business planning, enterprise awareness, bookkeeping, marketing etc.

The Prince's Youth Business Trust

Specialist business advice is given to young people aged up to 29 years who are keen to start a business. The Trust also provides grants, low-interest loans and training for potential entrepreneurs.
Contact the Trust on 020 7543 1234

Welfare Rights Service

Staff at Welfare Rights can advise you on your right to government benefits and can ensure you know your entitlement to financial support; they are highly trained to understand complex situations and government benefits. Check with your local authority or council for local telephone number, or the Citizens' Advice Bureau.

Things

Certain things have been found to have a positive effect on your ability to make a change in your life – here are the best.

Cultivating a positive, resourceful attitude

Some people are naturally positive, even optimistic; others may be more negative and pessimistic. Some people find themselves worn down by life and give up hoping and dreaming to avoid further disappointments. In earlier chapters, I argued that negative thinking is just a habit – you can equally cultivate the habit of positive thinking. This doesn't mean you have to be unrealistic, it just involves having a clear goal and taking steps to achieve it. This resourceful 'expectation mode' has a compelling outcome in everything we do – by a combination of planned choices and sheer serendipity, we make things happen for ourselves. Let's look at a real life example.

CASE STUDY
Lisa made the choice to look into training for playwork, with a view to eventually moving into hospital playwork. She decided to go along to a local after-school playclub and offer to volunteer for a few sessions. A week later she saw an advert for free playwork training offered by the local TEC. As a result of doing this, she heard about a higher-level college course she could study on a part-time basis.

You may think this was just a lucky break, but this kind of thing happens over and over again when people make a choice to make things happen in their lives. Harnessing the serendipitous in your life comes with making a clear choice to go for what you want. Being in a resourceful state means you have a heightened perception of what can help you achieve your goals, you know when to make your move, and you can deal with a setback or ambush without running for cover!

Dealing with a sit back
(No, this is not a spelling error!)

If you have ever watched a baby learning to walk you will know that there are stages of confidence, bumps, tears and exhilaration. Quite often, after a bad tumble, the baby sits back, as if thinking about it. The learning process can be extended or short lived, but there are a number of sit-backs before they take their first, unaided steps. Try using any occasional setbacks as your sit-back time – a short time out when you can assess how real the problem is, decide on alternatives or simply try again.

Making a dynamic plan

A dynamic plan is based on your own belief that you are worth a great deal, your own research into 'what is out there' for you and your wanting and yearning for a career change. The plan is the 'doing whatever it takes' part of your motivation, broken down into clear steps, and this plan has to be irresistible! Think of a game of snakes and ladders – there may be shortcuts (the ladders) and setbacks (the snakes). The most important thing is to stay in the game by continuing to throw the dice, and keeping your focus on the top square.

Taking the first step

Taking the first throw of the dice is just the first step, but you have to do it to get in the game. Making that first move can be exhilarating and scary at the same time, but once you have a game plan, don't put off starting to play!

Cognitive rehearsal and visualisation

We may not all be visual people, but picturing yourself doing something at some future point is an excellent way to programme yourself for success. If negative scenarios that we carry around can be powerful, why not make them positive? Cognitive rehearsal is just the technical, psychological term for doing this, and means that you think and see how you want something to be, in a meditative state, so that this picture/thought pattern becomes stronger than any negative expectations you may have. Here's a good example of cognitive rehearsal used to good effect.

Patrick had never performed well in interviews and had frequently experienced the dry mouth and shaking hands common to interview phobics. I helped him with some coaching: understanding the interview situation dynamic, the typical questions, his own body language etc, talked him through a relaxation technique that covered dealing with the panic symptoms and helped him to create a positive visualisation of how it could really be. In the five-minute relaxation, he fixed this new picture in his memory. He agreed to practise the technique every day for the week before his interview. On the day itself he was able to flash this picture into his mind whenever he thought of panicking and it calmed and focused him. His interview performance was 100 per cent better and he was offered the job. If you want to try this for yourself, this is how it goes.

Positive visualisation and relaxation technique

- Make sure you are in a comfortable, quiet, warm place, lying or sitting down.
- Take some time to stretch and tense each part of your body, finishing by letting go all tension.
- Imagine yourself at the top of a flight of stairs and start counting backwards from ten to one as you walk slowly down these stairs.
- When you get to the bottom of the stairs, visualise any emotional baggage you may have with you. You may see a rucksack on your back or be holding two suitcases. Fill this baggage with all the concerns or negative feelings you may be carrying around with you, and then leave it at the bottom of the stairs.
- Now start to see yourself getting ready to do the thing you may be scared of. Project a picture of yourself looking, feeling and sounding confident. Pay attention to the detail, your confident body language, posture, speech, facial mannerisms. Breathe in, hold this confident picture and 'fix' it in your mind. Breathe out and experience this feeling throughout your body.
- After a short pause, return in your mind to the bottom of the stairs, decide whether you want to retrieve the baggage (you probably don't!) and slowly move up the stairs counting from one to ten. Take a moment to come round before you open your eyes.
- Try practising some positive visualisation on a regular basis and you will find yourself in a more permanent positive mindset and people around you will notice this. In addition, you will find that serendipity takes place and you are more likely to reach out for the things you want, because you have already seen them as possible in your visualisation. Just try it!

Meaningful goal setting

Setting meaningful career goals is very much like playing a team game. In sport there are obvious, physical goals such as scoring; the less tangible goal of winning; and perhaps the personal, physical goal of keeping fit. For your career you may have the very obvious, tangible goal of earning more money, and the less tangible goal of feeling better about yourself or using your real potential. It's important to look beyond the mere physical to your real emotional goals, as although they link together the latter can be more powerful in motivating you. If it helps, visualise the goal post as what you want to happen and surround it with all your goals, both physical and emotional.

Finally, remember that your goals can and will change, so be ready to reassess what you want at regular intervals and refocus if necessary. The trick is to keep your eye on the ball and on the game, and enjoy it and keep your goal in sight at the same time! Remember that if you enjoy the game and find it exhilarating you are more likely to attain your goal.

A quick goal setting exercise

First stage

Try and do the first stage very quickly in an instinctive, 'off the top of your head' way. Take a blank piece of paper, head it 'Everything I want' and start writing with a timer set for one minute. Write quickly and without too much thought. Do not stop and analyse what you are writing and do not worry about how impossible some of the list might seem.

Second stage

Look down the list, read each item carefully and let your mind wander a little. You will find some surprises on the list — your subconscious may be trying to tell you something! Leave the list on one side for a day but think about what you wrote in any quiet moments you have. Still don't try to analyse it.

Third stage

Look down the list and order it according to the most important and the least important 'wants'. Look at each one in turn and analyse whether this want is an 'end' want or a 'means' want. Here's an example. Steven may have four top wants on his list, which may be:

1. I want a car.
2. I want a great job.

3. I want to earn good money.
4. I want to leave a footprint in the sand.

(1) may be an end want if he just wants a car because he loves cars, but if he wants a car to impress his friends, make life easier or to prove that he has made it, then it is probably a means want! Getting a car for Steven may be a means to the end of feeling good about himself.

(2) is probably a means want; it is likely that he wants a great job to feel successful or use his potential; the end will be feeling successful, or whatever he gains from being in a great job.

(3) is probably also a means want, as money is generally about security, success or power, which are the end wants.

(4) is generally an end want, as it is general and metaphorical; he may want to feel that what he does matters to someone or that he has made a difference, that his life has a purpose.

When you look through your list you may discover that you have all means wants, but if you analyse them you will discover what your ends might be. If you have lots of vague end wants only, then break them down into what the means wants could be.

Once you have your prioritised list of end and means wants you need to choose the first three in each list to focus on and research. You will then be able to decide whether these are real wants or whether you need to delete them from your list. After researching, you will have to set goals for each true and achievable want; you will decide the goal and then devise a strategy working back from your goal that will take you step by step. Remember that you can plan interim goals to keep you motivated. You may find that you are working towards several different goals; or, if you have had moderate success in your life by going with the flow, you can incorporate this into your goal setting. If you know what you want you will probably be looking in the right direction when the flow comes along.

Surrounding yourself with positive people

You may find that you gravitate towards positive people, probably because you recognise how fulfilling life can be with a positive mindset. Positive people are life enhancing, they fill you up, they laugh a lot – often at themselves – they appreciate people around them. Decide to be a positive person and believe in the power of the human spirit. Be appreciative of those around you and seek out other positive people as friends and colleagues; they will enrich your life.

Believing you can get what you want

Some of us, deep down, do not really believe that we can get what we want. It may be that as part of our upbringing we were told not to hope too much, and so not be too disappointed. (Many of my clients have completely lost the belief that they can get what they want by the age of 15.) It is hard to change a deeply ingrained belief, and the truth is that the wanting alone probably does set you up for failure. Knowing what you want is one thing; doing something to get what you want is about action, and that action feeds your belief.

Working out what motivates you

We are all motivated in different ways, and it is worth working out our optimum motivational situation so that we can use the same strategy to motivate ourselves in the future. Think of a time in your life when you were extremely motivated and analyse what the trigger was for this. If you can discover the stimulus for your motivation you can use this to motivate you today. You can also work out why your motivation might be failing you in some way.

It may help if I give you an example from my own life. When my children were little they ran to me one day to tell me that a friend of theirs had been locked in a tennis court by some teenagers. I ran to the tennis court, not a little worried about how I would deal with the situation. However, on arriving at the courts and seeing this 8-year-old boy locked in, with tears running down his face, I was possessed of a rage that surprised me. I marched towards the teenagers with such conviction and power of speech that they visibly backed away from me; one quickly unlocked the gate of the courts and they moved away in a thoroughly shamefaced way.

Afterwards I felt as if I had experienced an out of body experience, as I barely remembered what I had said or done. I just knew that I had felt invincible. My motivation, I realise now, was a sense of injustice and the fact that I abhor bullying. The trigger was a strong emotion, and all rationality went out the window. I now know that I can trust a strong feeling to be my motivator – it might be enthusiasm, a need for security or the need to protect someone else. Finding out your own motivational strategy and the trigger that works for you is vital, so take the time to discover this, and your progress towards your goal will be all the quicker.

Remember that using all the resources of help that are available makes sense, because doing it on your own is lonely and hard graft.

10 Career development/ self-development or unleashing your potential

When I visit employers as part of my job they often mention the inflexibility of some of their workforce as a key factor in their failure to clinch deals or create new business opportunities. Most companies need a multiskilled, adaptable workforce to cope with the demands of the changing environment of employment/business today. It seems that for some people, though, it is enough to carry on doing the same job in the same way; they may even complain about the sameness of their job while resisting change of any kind! Some employees are unwilling to undertake training courses, because it is perceived as extra workload without any financial incentive, but invariably when I do redundancy counselling people are eager to undertake training because their jobs are at risk. They often realise too late that it was their unwillingness to look up from the job in hand to the world outside, and the new need for lifelong learning, that may have caused the situation they find themselves in.

Keeping ahead of the game

This is essentially about fitness, in both senses of the word. Firstly, fitness is suitability for the work that needs to be done, not just what's in your job description. You will make yourself employable by fulfilling your job profile and a little bit more; keeping your eye on what makes your company successful and how you can play a significant part in this is as important as making a niche for yourself and developing your own skills and expertise.

This kind of fitness means that you volunteer for projects and offer to take on additional work *that interests you* to add to your personal portfolio of expertise. It also means that you take up any training that is available, sell the benefit of the organisation sponsoring you through training or pay for your own. They may see this training as proof of your commitment to the job or it may force them to reassess your value to them. It is bound to aid your career progress or open up opportunities elsewhere. Your own career plan is entirely based on self-interest, because you are relieving the employer of the responsibility for your career. You take charge, and this can be very empowering. Remember that, ultimately, the better you are, the more useful you will be to an employer, so the benefit goes both ways.

The second kind of fitness means that you are watching your own performance, improving your stamina and ability, continually striving to be fit and ready for anything that comes along. This type of fitness is vital for the changing world of employment.

Seeking out work opportunities

Within one employment situation lies a major source of alternative career opportunities. You will be connecting with both internal and external customers, who will take an impression of your skills and abilities. The internal customers are all your colleagues, from whom you can glean information about other job roles or opportunities within the firm, whether sideways or upwards, which would suit you better.

Secondly, in your contacts with external customers, you will come across job titles/roles that seem interesting to you and will be making contacts – use these to generate future jobs. If you are making a good impression with customer companies, you may find yourself headhunted!

Performance appraisals and getting what you want

A performance appraisal can be a negative experience, if it is just about reviewing what you have done. However, if you can review what you think the organisation needs and what you need, prior to the appraisal, you may be able to persuade your manager of some useful training you would like. Here is an example:

CASE STUDY
Isabel worked in a library but really wanted to move into human resource/personnel work. Training offered in recruitment was intended for middle management level. Isabel persuaded her manager that she had an interest in recruitment and would be able to stand in for interviews for library assistants if she had some training. Her manager saw the value of this, as recruitment and selection often took her away from essential work, and it would

be useful to have a stand in. The subsequent training was useful to Isabel as it confirmed her interest in this area and tempted her towards an evening IPD course, which helped her move her career in that direction.

Even the less interesting training courses, if offered by an employer, may have some eventual value to you, so consider all offers of training carefully, and particularly focus on any course that will give you a nationally recognised certification, for example NVQs, which can travel with you to another employer.

Making the job that you are in better

The most mundane job can be better if you decide to make the most of it, learn everything you can and do things, even if they are not in your job description. You may be accused of overkeenness, but life will be more interesting and you will uncover a launching pad to better things.

The launching pad may be quite unassuming – it may be that you offer to help train someone on the new computer system and find you have a gift for training. You may take additional computer courses in your own time and then, when the computer company that fitted your present company's computer system advertises for trainers, you decide to apply. You may just take off into a better job within your present company.

Networking and self-promotion

Networking is all about communicating with other people about what you do and finding out what they do. It means making a point of remembering people's names, from the cleaner to the managing director, and treating everyone with respect. It means helping colleagues out, if you can. It may also mean supporting and encouraging someone who is going through a bad patch, even if it is not your job to do so. It is about not being so work driven that you forget to notice the people around you. Most people like to chat about themselves, so networking can mean good listening. It is essentially about being nice to people around you – they may want to 'use' you one day, or you them. The word 'use' is the difficult part of this, but we all make use of people around us, and they make use of us. Don't get too hung up by the bad associations connected with the word.

Promoting yourself is another possibly uncomfortable concept. We don't want to be thought of as showing off, and we assume that that is what self-promotion is. It isn't. Self-promotion is the truth about what you can do. Showing off implies exaggerating what you can do. Self-promotion means that you might say, 'I can help you with that', if someone was explaining a problem within work. It might mean that you say, 'I would like to go for that training'. It does not mean being pushy, but it does mean not being a push-over! See *Projecting Your Skills at Work*, published by Trotman.

Recruitment agencies

Many serious job seekers have a mistaken view of recruitment agencies; firstly because they think that they only offer temporary, office-based work and that it would be costly to use their services. The facts are that good recruitment agencies do not charge to help you find a job because the employer-clients, to whom they provide a service, pay. Employers pay a charge to be introduced to you!

Secondly, many agencies specialise in particular types of work, from marketing, translating, teaching and IT to food or design companies, and many, many more. They can help you find permanent, contractual or temporary vacancies and all you need to do is register. Using recruitment agencies to activate your career plan can be of great benefit in introducing you to companies that choose only to recruit through agencies and may never advertise. Recruitment agencies advertise in Yellow Pages and on the Internet (see FRES on page 139); many will ask for your CV and wish to interview you.

Self-coaching/career coaching

Balance and a sense of perspective are important so, while you need to know the direction you want, you also have to make time for fun, and work can be fun. If you find reasonable enjoyment in what you do in an interim phase, plan for what you really want and enjoy the passing of time and the people around you while you execute your plan. If you are letting yourself be ground down by work and petty disagreements in the workplace you need to do some self-coaching to bring yourself out of this negative situation.

Start by focusing on the positives of your work and what you are gaining; then decide to ego stroke the warring people around you individually, and act as a mediator rather than a stirrer up of disagreements. Find some kind of retraining within or outside work that can uplift or inspire you. Manage your time so you work effectively, prioritising on a needs basis. If none of this seems to work, decide to explore opportunities with other employers or in other careers.

Self-coaching means that you talk to yourself, motivate yourself, challenge yourself to be the best you can, and generally everyone around you benefits.

It means you act as your own best friend and mentor, that you are tough on yourself when you come up with lame excuses for putting up with things or not going for what you want. If you find you are too easy on yourself then you may find it better to employ/hire a career or life coach to support and encourage you (see page 125).

The Internet

You will have heard about the wonders and terrors of the Internet, but for careers and job search purposes it is the wonders that are worth considering. There are some very good books on the Internet, and there are some excellent sites that can almost work miracles for career changers. Here are a few that I recommend, but start surfing to find out more. If you are a novice, take a taster course available at local colleges and some libraries. You will be enthralled!

Career Mosaic

http://www.careermosaic-uk.co.uk
This site has good employer information, a place where you can search for vacancies and somewhere you can 'post' your CV, via email or by cutting and pasting it to an assigned area.

Career Zone UK

http://www.careerzone-uk.com/
This site advertises 5000 online vacancies and can distribute your CV to recruitment agencies. Professional careers advisers are available to give guidance.

Careers Portal

http://www.careers-portal.co.uk
A links portal site dedicated to careers guidance with over 1700 links.

Careers Services National Association

http://www.careers-uk.com
This site has a list of all the UK careers services under contract to the DfEE, and may offer free or subsidised careers advice to adults.

Federation of Recruitment and Employment Services (FRES)

http://www.fres.co.uk/
This is a good site to connect with, so that you know about those recruitment agencies that work to a recognised code of practice. Phone 0800 320 588 for a list of member consultancies in your area.

Gis-a-job

http://www.gisajob.com/

This is a bright and appealing site that offers free job searches, free jobs by email and free CV storage.

Jobs Unlimited

http://www.jobsunlimited.co.uk

This is the Guardian job vacancy site with a wide range that you can browse through.

Monster Board UK

http://www.monsterboard.co.uk

This site offers a CV posting service that employers can browse through. There are 2000 job vacancies listed and it is possible to do regional and company searches.

Always be looking

It may be that once you get your dream job you relax and think 'That's it!' You may think it unsettling to be permanently looking around for better things – it doesn't need to be. Being self-aware means reviewing your own needs and desires on a regular basis, as these are bound to change; you will also need to be aware of the changing world of 'what's out there'. Being flexible and ready to change should be your new mindset, which will make you relatively flame proof whatever happens. Seek a little edge in your life and you will feel stretched and challenged. Remember that better things for you may not be paid work but voluntary work; it may be opting out and downshifting into something quite different, as long as it fits with your personal qualities and desires. Be sure that a sustained wanting, a passion and a desire plus real action will work to motivate you, however many career/life changes you make.

The wooden bridge

A final picture for you: a person is stepping tentatively across a wooden bridge. The bridge doesn't look too safe and there are a few slats missing. The person therefore spends the whole time focusing on their feet and the dangers of the bridge, only occasionally looking up to the blue of the sky and the vista on the other side of the bridge. Many of us are like that person, worrying about the dangers, expecting disaster, when it might be more useful to look up and enjoy the view. Looking down may feel safer, but looking up, around and forward is more uplifting.